"Chasing opportunities and sending countless follow-up emails didn't get me closer to my dream role, so I followed the advice in *Small Actions*. New opportunities started presenting themselves. I was also offered a promotion as my team looked at me in a different light. It's magical how the practical tips in this book helped me pivot my career within such a short time."

Anna Udartseva, Growth Associate, AlphaSights;
Host of Career Lesson podcast; ex-EY Consultant (U.K.)

"Sim masterfully weaves together a canvas of his observations about mindsets, skills, and behaviors that are important to every professional. *Small Actions* is a must read for those who want to make the most out of their life and career."

Frank Koo, Head of Asia Talent Solutions, LinkedIn

"*Small Actions* brings to life the lessons learned through Sim's remarkable career. It offers simple steps that can help any career-minded individual achieve greater growth and success."

Peter Healey, CEO, eFinancialCareers

"I like this book's effortless and insightful narration, and Sim's strong thought leadership on career strategies. Readers, from graduates to professionals, will find valuable advice to help them realize their potential."

Ani Filipova, former Chief Operating Officer,
Asia Treasury and Trade Solutions, Citi

"The small actions that you take by reading this book could really lead to your next big success."

Handi Kurniawan,
Group Head of Leadership and Academies Learning, Jardine Matheson

"A digestible, honest and personal handbook that I wish I had come across earlier."

Shakiru Okunade, Crude Oil Trading Analyst, Chevron

"Next time you are travelling for business meetings, you will not just relish the local food, but learn how to effectively use that to build your social capital."

Anil Ghelani, CFA, Senior Vice President, DSP Mutual Fund;
Vice Chairman, CFA Society India

"The small actions I took from reading Sim's advice opened up many doors. This book condenses his journey to becoming a powerful brand into simple steps to advance our careers and expand our networks, even for those who are just getting started."

Vanessa Ho, Instagram influencer, media personality

"Sim illustrates concepts that help readers jumpstart their careers with small actions."

Ian Loh, MBA candidate, Oxford University

"Not just for students, any working adult can benefit from this book's tips about career development and life, which are applicable both in and outside of the workplace. An easy read, yet flavorful, invigorating, and full of optimism!"

Enna Tan, Head, BIZCareers,
National University of Singapore Business School

"A comprehensive 'wisdom menu' served up for 21st century career journeys."

Shivendu Nadkarni, former Regional VP,
Kellogg's Asia-Pacific, Middle East and Africa

"Practical! I especially like how Sim incorporates his life experiences."

Zubaidah (Zuby) Osman, Head of Centre for Excellence,
Great Eastern Life Assurance

"This book is the result of failures, perseverance and many years of self-development. It will open your eyes on how to succeed in a simple, efficient and sustainable way."

William Tohmé, Senior Regional Head, Middle East and North Africa,
CFA Institute

"Sim shares his wisdom on how we can be creators of our own destiny and success."

Christina Wüllner, student, University of Mannheim, Germany

"*Small Actions* takes you on a journey through Sim's life and career, and translates his stories into actionable tips that quickly pay big dividends for your own career."

Chris Mattia, LinkedIn Learning Instructor, California

SMALL ACTIONS

Leading Your Career to Big Success

SMALL ACTIONS

Leading Your Career to Big Success

Eric Sim
Institute of Life

Simon Mortlock

World Scientific

V JERSEY · LONDON · SINGAPORE · BEIJING · SHANGHAI · HONG KONG · TAIPEI · CHENNAI · TOKYO

Published by

World Scientific Publishing Co. Pte. Ltd.

5 Toh Tuck Link, Singapore 596224

USA office: 27 Warren Street, Suite 401-402, Hackensack, NJ 07601

UK office: 57 Shelton Street, Covent Garden, London WC2H 9HE

Library of Congress Cataloging-in-Publication Data
Names: Sim, Eric, author. | Mortlock, Simon, author.
Title: Small actions : leading your career to big success / Eric Sim, Simon Mortlock.
Description: New Jersey : World Scientific, [2022]
Identifiers: LCCN 2021043206 | ISBN 9789811232572 (hardcover) |
    ISBN 9789811233852 (paperback) | ISBN 9789811232589 (ebook) |
    ISBN 9789811232596 (ebook other)
Subjects: LCSH: Career development. | Success in business.
Classification: LCC HF5381 .S6115 2022 | DDC 650.1--dc23
LC record available at https://lccn.loc.gov/2021043206

British Library Cataloguing-in-Publication Data
A catalogue record for this book is available from the British Library.

Cover design by Tom Butler, thebutlerdidit.co.uk
Profile photo of Eric Sim by Jake Gaba, Schwarzman Scholar, New York

For any available supplementary material, please visit
https://www.worldscientific.com/worldscibooks/10.1142/12169#t=suppl

Desk Editor: Nicole Ong

Typeset by Stallion Press
Email: enquiries@stallionpress.com

Printed in Singapore

Contents

Introduction
A Life of Small Actions

For much of my life and until quite recently, I suffered from an inferiority complex. If you saw my high school report card and read my teachers' assessment of me, you'd know I was a shy boy who lacked social skills, was academically weak, and didn't excel at sport.

Ever since those school days, I've been trying to overcome my sense of inferiority, and figure out how to achieve success. One of my earliest and most enduring strategies was to build up knowledge across a range of subjects. I attended a plethora of courses — from interior design, to photography, to positive psychology — as I tried to overcompensate for my insecurities. I now have a huge folder filled to the brim with certificates. While my newly gained knowledge did help to build my confidence, my feelings of not being good enough never completely went away.

The day I finally put my inferiority complex to rest was when I gave an online speech to Oxford University students and alumni. I switched on the main light in my home studio and sat down in front of my camera. The moderator, an MBA candidate from the university's business school, welcomed me and read out my biography. Before I started my speech on demonstrating thought leadership, she asked me:

"Eric, last month, you made two of LinkedIn's lists for its content creators: LinkedIn Top Voices for Singapore and LinkedIn Spotlight for China. Congratulations! I also understand that you had a busy job as a banker, but still found time to work as an associate adjunct professor, social media opinion leader, and keynote speaker. How did you manage to be successful at all these things in your career?"

It was a good question, and came just two months after I'd been asked a similar one when delivering a talk to EMBA students at Chicago Booth. It made me think that I must have done something right in my career. Why else would students from these top schools invite me to present, and bother listening to my session when it didn't count towards a course credit? How had I (in the students' own words) become a "success"?

These were challenging questions, and I knew that providing a short answer during a webinar wasn't sufficient. I needed to explore the concept of success, and how to achieve it, in much greater depth. With this goal now in my mind, I decided to team up with Simon Mortlock — a journalist, editor and content manager I know, who specializes in careers and employment — to write this book.

A Gradual Career Journey

As I began planning what to put in these pages, I looked back on my life and tried to uncover the origins of the career success that the students were so interested in. When I examined the milestones in my career, I realized that I'm not a particularly courageous person. I've never made any really bold and dangerous decisions, like quitting my job without having another one to go to. What I have done, however, is taken many small actions over the course of my career and my life, the accumulation of which has ultimately led me to success. My career journey has been gradual and ongoing rather than sudden and dramatic. Small actions pay dividends over time, not immediately.

Just before graduating from university with an engineering degree, I bumped into a classmate who told me about a campus recruitment talk by a Singapore an bank that he'd attended. I'd missed the event, but I sent an unsolicited application letter to the bank anyway, which led to me getting a job offer. If it weren't for the small action of writing that letter, my decades-long career in banking would have been dead from the outset because up until then I'd been rejected by all the financial institutions I'd applied to.

My career has since brought me to live in Hong Kong, Shanghai and London, so besides Singapore (where I am now), the settings of this book also span across international locations. I was based in Hong Kong on three separate occasions, so I know that city particularly well and it provides a backdrop to several of the stories I'm about to tell you.

What Success Means to Me

By taking small actions, I've achieved career success by most conventional standards, such as having a high salary and a senior title. But to me, that's not what success is actually about. Yes, money is important, but that's because you need a good amount of it to achieve long-term financial independence, not because you need an excess of it to buy an exotic car or lead an extravagant lifestyle.

I believe that measuring success purely in terms of income and seniority is far too narrow. To be truly successful, we also need to feel fulfilled and happy most of the time. By this definition, a high-ranking job is no guarantor of success. CEOs may not feel happy because they don't have much privacy in their lives and face restrictions on what they can and cannot say. Sometimes their personal values may conflict with the interests of the organization they represent.

We should also stop segregating our career and our life so clearly. If we're not happy in one, we won't be happy in the other. That's why I recommend in this book that we try to incorporate our interests into our jobs, and we practise "work-life integration" instead of work-life balance.

Choose Your Own Small Actions

So what small actions could you take that could lead you to success and happiness? This book contains 66 practical examples that have worked well for me, the students I teach, and the mid-career executives I coach. I've grouped the bite-size chapters into 11 core themes: from increasing your influence and building your personal brand, to dealing with challenges, and demonstrating your leadership. Each chapter stands on its own, so you can explore the book in whatever order appeals to you, although you're likely to discover more insights if you read the chapters in sequence.

No matter how you approach your reading, there is no need to carry out all 66 small actions. Doing just a few of the suggestions in this book is enough to set you in the right direction. And you'll find that your first action naturally leads you to the next one, so very soon you'll be on your way to achieving big success in your career.

Part One

It's Your Career: Plan It, Manage It

01
What is a Combo Specialist?

I regularly advise the next generation about their career ambitions. No matter their degree or industry, many young people I chat with ask me this binary question: "Should I be a generalist or a specialist in my career?" I reply that it's best not to be pigeonholed into either extreme.

As industries are disrupted by technology and big trends outside of your control, your career will inevitably go through periods of drastic change. You should avoid becoming a generalist because your lack of in-depth knowledge means you could be replaced very easily. But you don't want to be a one-dimensional specialist because you run the risk of becoming obsolete when your industry gets disrupted. Instead, you should aim to be a "combo specialist".

Let me illustrate this by using the combo meal at McDonald's as an analogy. This typically consists of a burger, a pack of French fries and a glass of Coke. The burger is your primary specialization, the fries are your secondary specialization, and the Coke is your interest. I've had several combos during my career.

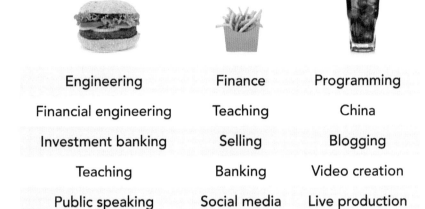

Engineering	Finance	Programming
Financial engineering	Teaching	China
Investment banking	Selling	Blogging
Teaching	Banking	Video creation
Public speaking	Social media	Live production

When I got my first job in banking after graduating with an engineering degree, my burger was engineering, my fries were my financial skills, and my Coke was computer programming. I had to quickly learn about financial markets to make finance my burger. While I wasn't confident enough socially at that time to perform well in foreign-exchange sales, my bosses noted the high quality of my analytical work. I was given more tasks that involved analyzing the financial markets. I also used my interest in computer programming to automate repetitive tasks.

As my career progressed, financial engineering became my burger. I was able to structure and price complex financial products. Teaching was my fries, while my interest in China was my Coke…so I ended up teaching my colleagues in China about financial engineering.

After several years in Singapore, I moved to Shanghai and then Hong Kong to cover Chinese corporate and institutional clients. Offering investment banking solutions suitable for mainland customers was my burger, my selling skills were my fries, and my interest in blogging became my Coke.

As a university lecturer, my teaching skills are my burger. But I also add extra value (i.e. fries) by incorporating lessons from my banking deals (without mentioning clients' names) into my banking and finance lectures, so students get a taste of real-life transactions. I've recently developed an interest in making videos (my Coke), which comes in handy because students are increasingly watching lectures online.

My university work has led me to become a professional speaker (my burger). I give talks to large audiences on career and life skills, and I'm able to charge speaking fees. Many of my gigs were moved online during the pandemic, but I turned this to my advantage. Before COVID-19, conference producers could get attendees by hosting their sessions at fancy hotels and offering networking opportunities. But with online events, organizers rely much more on the brand names of the speakers to pull in the crowds. When the pandemic started, I already had a strong social media presence (my fries) to help attract people to webinars. My interest in using a live production switcher (my Coke) allows me to deliver higher quality productions. I get more work as a speaker because of this combo skill set.

The three main benefits of becoming a combo specialist are:

— You can gradually change your specializations into new areas as you combine your core and secondary skills with your interests.
— You have a competitive edge over one-dimensional specialists.
— You enjoy your job more because you're incorporating your interests into your work (read more in Chapter 6).

If you're an engineer, you could be even more in demand if you add design skills. And if you like photography, that could be your Coke. Create your own combo to suit your career ambitions. Many industries will be disrupted — whether by technology, a pandemic or something else — and having a combo skill set will help you cope with changes that come your way because you'll be nimbler and more adaptable, and have more to offer your employer. Be a combo specialist; be unique.

02

Why You Need a Second Career

It's difficult to derive everything we want in life from just one job because most of us are looking for that elusive blend of money, meaning and happiness. Your day job is bound by an employment contract, which is like an SPA (sale and purchase agreement) in an M&A (mergers and acquisitions) transaction. There's a buyer (you) and there's a seller (your employer). You sell your time and services in exchange for money. But in this transaction, there's no mention of either meaning or happiness, so it's unfair and unrealistic to expect your employer to deliver all three essential elements of your life.

Instead, I try to get each component from a different job or interest: banking gives me money; teaching gives me meaning; and speaking and writing give me happiness. My conference speeches take me to new places, where I learn about other cultures, while blogging creates opportunities to make high-quality connections.

I'm not alone in doing a broad range of activities as I seek a fulfilling life. I'm meeting more and more professionals who are taking on new tasks away from their core job. I'm not talking about the old trend of people quitting the sector they work in altogether; I'm referring to those who are staying in the same industry while pursuing an additional career at the weekend, after work and during their annual leave. Let me first explain why you might want to have a side job, and then explore how you can make a success of one.

Why Have a Second Career?

Your Skills Won't be Wasted

Most people have multiple skills and talents. In my view, it's a pity that you only use your intelligence and knowledge within one sector.

You Get Fulfilment

Many industries, including banking, law and consulting, can be cutthroat and political, especially during economic downturns. Even if you receive a high salary and bonus, you may not get fulfilment from your job. Having a side gig allows you to have more meaning in your life.

You Mix with Different People

One of the main advantages of an additional career is that you have opportunities to talk to people who you wouldn't typically come across in your sector. I find it fascinating to have conversations about non-financial topics. I frequently mix with marketing people to chat about digital marketing, and with academics to discuss education.

Your Main Career Improves

Your side gig can help you perform better in your day job. Because of my work with mainland universities, Chinese clients regarded me not just as a finance professional but as a teacher, which is a respected position in China. Some of my students even referred their bosses to me. Your second job can get you a foot in the door with people who would otherwise be tricky to meet. If you own a restaurant on the side, for example, host special meals for your day-job colleagues.

Extra Income

It shouldn't be your primary objective, but some additional income is always welcome.

How to Make a Success of Your Side Job

Try It at Your Company First

Your colleagues are a great testing ground for your second-job idea. If they don't like what you're doing, you should probably look for ways to improve. If you want to set up a baking business, see if your co-workers actually enjoy eating your cakes. If you're interested in public speaking, take advantage of speaking sessions at your firm. If you're a budding singer, find out if your company runs an annual talent show.

Profile Yourself on Social Media

I've learned from experience that being active on social media can increase the chances of business opportunities coming your way. As I'll explain in Part 2 of this book, LinkedIn has been a highly effective platform for me. I let my followers know that I'm a speaker, lecturer and writer as well as a banker. Organizations such as the Chartered Financial Analyst (CFA) Institute have engaged me to speak and teach as a result.

Get Support From Your Boss

It's essential to have a good relationship with your boss, otherwise they might use your side gig against you. You want your manager to be thinking, "you're active outside of work and yet still perform so well here". I was lucky that my managers were very supportive.

Ensure Your Day Job Always Takes Priority

It's possible that your side gig could eventually become your full-time career, but while you're still employed, under no circumstances should your company think that you're not committed to your work. I used up much of my annual leave to teach and speak, which further ensured that my bosses couldn't fault my commitment to my day job.

Charge a Fee and Declare It

If you get paid, you know it's a proper side job and not just a hobby. During the first few years of my teaching, I didn't ask to be paid because I was new to teaching and I wanted to avoid the hassle of declaring my fee to my company's compliance and HR departments. After gaining enough teaching experience, I decided to charge a fee, and went through the long and painful approval process imposed by my employer. It was worth the time and effort! The fee proved to myself that I could cut it as a lecturer.

I hope you'll start thinking about taking up a second career yourself. Make it something that inspires you, and gives you the meaning and happiness that your day job might not provide.

03

Bosses

After completing my master's in the U.K., I returned to Singapore. Unfortunately, the 1997 Asian financial crisis had struck by the time I got back! The job market suddenly took a big turn for the worse, and I had to abandon my plans to become a derivatives structurer.

Forced to change tack, I decided to apply for risk management vacancies instead. I managed to secure job offers from two banks, one of which was larger and more prestigious than the other. In the end, I opted for the role at the smaller bank and took a position that was more junior than I was hoping for. Why did I settle for something that seemed, on the surface at least, to be second best? It was because I thought that my boss, Prasanna, at the smaller bank would support my personal development over the longer term. My initial assumption paid off: Prasanna helped me build a strong foundation for my career.

The Benefits of Working for a Boss Who Believes in You

If you're finding it challenging to land a job in your dream company, try instead to work for a boss who believes in you, regardless of the role you're offered and the size of the firm. What are the advantages of working for this kind of manager? Here are some of the main ones:

You Become More Willing to Try New Things

Having a good boss makes you bolder and more innovative. While I was working for Prasanna I published an article in a trade journal about bank capital. How did I have the guts to do this as a fairly junior employee? I had my manager's blessing and I knew he would back me if I received criticism for the article. If you don't have a supportive boss, you become more risk averse yourself and end up doing the same things over and over again until your skills become obsolete.

Your Job is More Enjoyable

A boss who believes in you will recognize your strengths and let you perform more interesting and enjoyable tasks. In doing this, they make your whole job more pleasant and you look forward to coming to work each day. Prasanna saw that I had skills in VBA programming, so he asked me to help set up a risk management monitoring spreadsheet for the bank's newly established exotic options trading desk. I loved working on this additional assignment, so I became more enthusiastic about my role at the bank.

You Get More Opportunities

When I arrived back in Singapore after my failed London job hunt, I never expected to return to the British capital less than a year later. But Prasanna had faith in my abilities and seconded me to London for six months. After London, I spent another six months in Hong Kong. Sending me overseas wasn't an easy decision for Prasanna: he could have given these sought-after secondments to someone else, and he had to arrange cover for my job in Singapore. But thanks to him, I was now on the path to having an international career. I was tearful when Prasanna resigned, such was his impact on my life. In our careers, many of us prioritize pay and working for a big brand, but having a boss who believes in you is more important as it allows you to grow in confidence and fulfill your potential.

How to Outlast a Bad Boss

While we should always strive to work for supportive managers, sometimes this just isn't possible. You can count yourself lucky if you have one or two good bosses in your entire career. Bosses can be bad for a number of reasons, so I'm not going to tell you how to cope with every different type of manager you could ever come across. But I will give you my thoughts on how to outlast a bad boss, with the ultimate aim of being transferred within your company rather than moving to a new employer. If you quit your job because you dislike your manager, you're bound to end up working for someone even worse at your next firm.

Help Other Departments

If you help your colleagues (at all levels) in other departments and other countries, they'll get to like you and they may inform you of job openings in their teams. If you're on holiday in a city where your company has an office, drop by to say hello. Having relationships across different parts of your organization could ultimately lead to an internal transfer and free you from working for your current manager.

Build Good Relationships with Your Boss's Bosses

Your line manager may be threatened by you and your ideas, but the bosses two or more ranks above you won't be because they're too senior. It's important to build strong relationships with them because they control your company's overall strategy and could assign you to another team if that suits their plans. You'll last longer at your firm if you have at least one person in the upper ranks who supports you and could also help manage any conflict between you and your line manager.

Make it a point to talk to senior people during company events, and offer to take them out if they're visiting your country from overseas. To get to know your big bosses, you should develop some signature skills (see Chapter 7) because they're unlikely to talk to you about your day job without involving your immediate supervisor. Perhaps you're renowned internally for making training videos, so managers throughout your company come to you when they want to shoot a video. I became a Mac fanatic early on in my career and whenever someone at my firm wanted to buy a Mac, they'd ask me for advice. I even went to a senior manager's house to teach him how to use one, so my signature skill helped me build relationships with both juniors and seniors at my firm.

Keep on Performing Well

Having a bad manager is no excuse for performing poorly. Regardless of your boss, you can't let your standards drop because your company might just get rid of you. It's best to be patient. Even if you don't get transferred yourself, your boss could resign, be promoted or join another team. Moreover, if you're a top performer, your relationship with your boss may even improve over time as they grow to recognize your value to the team.

Research the Boss Before You Accept the Role

I try to work for people I've already met and got to like and respect, but that's not always possible, especially at the start of our careers. During the recruitment process, many of us are too focused on landing the job and ensuring the pay and title are good enough, so we forget to research the boss. Be sure to ask your potential manager searching questions during the interview, although they'll probably be on their best behavior and may not reveal their true personality. If you want to know what the manager is really like, you should talk to people who've worked with them before. Your manager will be background checking you, so you should do the same to them. Even if you have no choice but to accept the job, you'll at least know what's in store for you and how to pull the right strings with your new boss.

Know what to expect from your manager before you join their team. Once you're in the role, build up your internal networks and become a connector across departments. If your relationship with your immediate boss turns sour, you need other people in the organization to help open up opportunities for you.

04

Be Your Own CEO

I like to think of myself as the CEO of Eric Sim Consulting, a firm with only one staff member: me. I consider the companies I've worked for not as my employers but as my "clients", who pay me a "consulting fee" rather than a salary for my time and services. When I'm in a consultancy mindset, my motivations are different to those of an employee. Imagining myself as a CEO means I want to build long-term relationships with my "clients", so I agree to do work that's not strictly within my job scope, such as organizing events and cross-selling other departments' products. This may take me away from my main job, but it's good for my "client" relationships, so it could open up new opportunities in the future.

If you want to be your own CEO, you must be prepared to spend your own money to enhance your career. For example, you can't always rely on your company to send you on the training programs that you think will boost your skills and keep you up to date with industry trends. The most prestigious firms can even be tightfisted when it comes to smaller expenses, such as buying quality stationery. I purchased my own pens for much of my career, while a colleague of mine bought his own desk lamp to make up for the poor lighting above his seat in the office.

Quite a lot of professionals I've come across, however, are reluctant to part with their own money if the expense is associated with work, even if that's just buying a mouse pad or a footrest to make their workspace more comfortable. Because they think like employees rather than consultants, they expect their companies to provide everything that's related to their job.

Having a CEO mentality will come in handy when you hit a roadblock in your career because you'll be willing to spend money and/or time to help overcome the problem. Let me share four cases that illustrate the benefits of acting like a CEO of your own consulting company.

The Bootcamp that Changed My Life

At the beginning of my career, my life insurance agent told me about a motivational bootcamp in Malaysia that he and hundreds of other agents from his firm were attending. The ABC (awareness before change) course focused on how to build resilience in the face of rejection, and he said it would turn anyone into a superman or superwoman, able to take on seemingly impossible tasks. The training sounded great and I knew it would benefit me in the long term, but it wasn't directly related to my junior job in risk management. My company would never sponsor me, but the moment I put on my CEO hat I knew that I had to ask my agent to sign me up. I paid for the course and took five days of annual leave to attend it. The money was well spent because the course set me up for the rest of my career: it improved my teamwork skills and made me more resilient and better able to cope with rejection and change.

I was the only person not from the insurance firm among the hundreds of agents who participated in the grueling program, which ran from dawn to dusk under the command of a tough ex-army colonel. We left our dorms early each morning for a timed run, and by the end of the week even the slowest person in the group saw their performance improve, encouraged by the rest of us. We also read mantras like "for things to change, I must change first" about a hundred times a day, and listened to songs like *I Believe I Can Fly* and *He Ain't Heavy, He's My Brother*. We laughed and cried together — there was some motivational brainwashing, but I enjoyed it. It changed my life!

Jack's Unfortunate Email

Jack was working for one of the Big Four auditing firms in the U.K. when an important American client told him to take on some urgent additional work. Jack decided not to prioritize this new request ahead of his existing tasks for other clients, and he wrote a nicely worded email to his boss outlining his reasons. The manager understood his justification, but Jack had made an error: he'd copied the U.S. client into the email. Jack freaked out! He couldn't sleep for two days. In the meantime, his firm wasn't helping to get him out of the mess.

When Jack asked for my advice, I told him to assert himself and act like he was CEO of Jack Consulting. Instead of hoping for salvation as an employee, CEO Jack could instead turn his problem into an opportunity. I suggested that he take two days' annual leave, buy a plane ticket to the U.S. at his own expense, and visit the client to say sorry in person. The client would see that Jack was sincere since he'd paid for everything himself. Jack could also consider buying a small gift for the client to add extra clout to his apology.

In the end, the client didn't react as badly to the email as Jack had initially feared, so he didn't need to visit the U.S. But the realization that he had a potential route to sort out his problems was an enormous psychological relief for Jack: his sleep immediately returned to normal and from that point on he understood the value of spending his own money to help his own career. Jack remains at his firm today and still works with the same client.

Putting on a Show in Shanghai

My regional boss asked me if I'd like to coordinate a three-day offsite event in Shanghai for CFOs of some of the most important corporate clients in Asia. This was no easy assignment: it involved organizing training, a tourism excursion, and a big dinner for senior managers from my bank and 30 CFOs from across Asia. It would take me away from revenue generating and I'd have to do some of the work in my spare time. But as CEO of Eric Sim Consulting, I gladly accepted the challenge as I realized there would be long-term benefits. There has to be both give and take in our careers: if you do extra jobs outside your KPIs, your boss will be more willing to take care of you in the future.

I set about my tasks with relish. I searched for music from old Shanghai and found a CD called Shanghai Jazz, a modern take on classic 1920s songs. The tracks were mesmerizing, which inspired me to plan the whole CFO dinner around the album. I managed to get a local jazz singer to perform at the dinner, which we turned into a glamorous jazz night. Every guest received a copy of the CD as a door gift along with Chinese costumes to wear for the big night. The evening was spectacular and set new standards for my firm's client events. Clients were impressed and the firm's relationships with them were strengthened. For me, learning how to organize client events and getting to know my bank's sales heads from several Asian countries was well worth the time I'd spent arranging everything.

Evelyn's Timid Boss

At the start of the COVID-19 pandemic, Evelyn, a junior finance professional, volunteered to set up a Zoom meeting for her team members. Zoom offered a free service for calls up to 40 minutes, so to save the trouble of dialing back in once meetings passed that time limit, Evelyn asked her manager if she could take out a three-month subscription for US$45. The boss replied that he would have to wait and check with his own manager because video conferencing wasn't specifically covered by the company's expenses policy. Evelyn's boss should have instead put on his CEO hat and told her right away to subscribe via his own credit card. Even if he didn't get reimbursed by the company, he should have been willing to spend the small amount of US$45 to make communicating more convenient for his team. In my opinion, if managers can't make that kind of decision, they're not fit to be managers.

Your employer primarily looks after its own corporate interests, so you shouldn't wait for it to cater to your individual needs because you may be waiting a long time. As a CEO, you should buy your own subscriptions, gadgets, and training courses and work out your own solutions to career problems. If you come across a product or service that will help you in your job, just go ahead and get it without worrying whether your manager will approve the expense or not.

There's a lot of justified hype about the startup sector these days, but you don't need to become an entrepreneur to take charge of your career. Thinking like a CEO means being *intrapreneurial* instead: you're essentially running your own business within your current company, and you're making bolder, more innovative decisions as a result. Your job also takes on a different meaning when you adopt the perspective of a CEO. You get a greater sense of autonomy, which makes your work more meaningful and fulfilling.

One of my LinkedIn followers, Edouard, recently described how his career took a positive turn when he read an article of mine and decided to become his own CEO. All it took was a change of mindset.

The following is written in the first person by Edouard:

I went through many ups and downs in my job during 2019. I felt unexcited about some of my work, lacked a clear direction of where my role was heading, and didn't have a solid understanding of how I fit into the organization. In a nutshell, I felt lost. I focused more on the aspects of my work that I disliked than on what I could learn from the job. I remember vividly the time when I began occasionally working from home. I'd had enough of always going to the office — sitting at the same desk and looking at the same things every day — especially given the solo nature of my role. I could go for days without talking to anyone.

But when I was working outside the office, I no longer felt like an employee. I felt as if I'd been hired as a consultant, going out to lunch on my own time (within reasonable hours), working for the company remotely, and popping into the office once in a while. However, I wasn't too sure whether this "consulting feeling" was justified. Did it make me look like someone who didn't really care about being an integral part of the organization? It was right around this time I came across an article by Eric that, coincidentally, touched on this exact issue, and explained how he had made his jobs more bearable. "Think of yourself as CEO of your own consulting company" was one of the subheadings.

I felt relieved! My entire mindset shifted from pessimism and self-doubt, to confidence and excitement. I approached mundane tasks with an uplifted spirit, telling myself that I had a fiduciary responsibility to get the work done for my "client" (i.e. my employer), regardless of how I felt about the tasks. I found I was in a better position than a "real" consultant because at least I didn't need to worry about chasing people for money and projects getting canceled. All I needed to worry about was getting the work done; the rest was already taken care of.

(Continued)

(Continued)

This mentality also helped me solidify my work ethic, both for myself and in the eyes of others. I happily volunteered to take on extra work, and became even more proactive at sharing and executing new ideas. Ultimately, my new attitude strengthened my leadership style. I'm now someone who uplifts and empowers people around him by exhibiting constant energy; not someone who complains and approaches things with negativity. This little mindset shift, this "small action", has helped me in a big way.

05

Great Opportunities Come at Inconvenient Times

After four years in Shanghai and Hong Kong, I returned to Singapore to be closer to my family. For me, Singapore is home — a comfortable place to live and work — and I felt I'd made the most out of my time abroad. Tired of living in rented apartments overseas, where I needed my landlord's permission just to hang up a picture, I moved into my own place in Singapore and renovated it to suit my own needs. I also bought a car, and was ready to stay in Singapore for good.

Life was going smoothly in Singapore when, less than two years after my return, a top-tier bank in Hong Kong offered me a job opportunity. This bank had a bigger platform and a wider range of products for me to serve my clients. I would get involved in larger deals, meet CEOs of bigger companies, and gain even more exposure to Greater China. I also knew some of the bank's senior management, which would be a great help for me as I adjusted to my new working environment.

But I wasn't keen to move again so soon after I'd left Hong Kong. The role was covering the Asian region, so I tried to convince the hiring manager to base me in Singapore and I promised him I would fly to Greater China every other week. He said "no!" So I then rented out my Singapore apartment, sold my car, and relocated to Hong Kong to take up the job. In hindsight my manager was right: it's far easier to travel to mainland cities from Hong Kong, and most of our business came from Greater China. My decision to move led to me staying in Hong Kong for seven years — and I'm glad I did. I got to work with many talented individuals, who helped to shape my career and life.

Alvin Starts Teaching Again

Alvin, the CEO of a $7 billion real estate fund, is another person who took up an opportunity even though the timing wasn't perfect. Alvin told Lee, a common friend of ours, about his desire to start teaching again after many years. One Friday evening, Lee came to my networking event and brought Alvin along to introduce him to me. Alvin shared with me that he used to teach in his spare time more than 10 years ago, but had given up because of the demands of his job. I could feel Alvin's desire to give teaching another go.

I've come across several people like Alvin over the years. I know that while they're interested in teaching, they usually won't make the effort or commitment to teach. So I tested Alvin, as I had tested the others. I invited him to make a guest presentation for 15 minutes during a lecture I was giving at a local university in Singapore that coming Sunday. Knowing that he's the CEO of a large company, I expected him to say he was busy, just like the other people who had come to me before him.

When he said he needed to think about it, I thought to myself, "why am I not surprised!" Alvin explained that the timing wasn't good for him because during that weekend he had to help his son prepare for his Primary School Leaving Exam, a life-changing test that decides the fate of many 12-year-old Singaporeans. The results of that exam determine which high school these kids will attend; and some schools are more prestigious than others. Alvin now had to balance his interest in teaching with the fate of his son. On Saturday late afternoon, he texted me that he and his wife had swapped timings for helping their son study. He'd now be available to attend my lecture and speak for 10 to 15 minutes about his career as a fund manager and the attributes he looks for when hiring people.

His speech was a success — the students loved it — and he wrote about it on social media. Several universities were delighted to read about this senior financial professional who enjoys teaching, and Alvin soon received invitations to teach at three more universities. Without making that last-minute and slightly inconvenient Sunday afternoon commitment, Alvin says he might not have renewed his passion for teaching and certainly wouldn't have gotten so many speaking and teaching assignments in quick succession.

Not all of us would seize the moment like Alvin did. Too often we come up with excuses when opportunities are presented to us: we'll do it when we have more time, or feel more confident in our abilities. But there's never a perfect time to grab great opportunities, and if we wait too long our chance may never return. Professionals who refuse overseas transfers during a downturn may live to regret their decision. If they try to move only when market conditions improve, opportunities may not be there anymore because they'll be facing much stronger competition for jobs.

Had I not been willing to relocate to Hong Kong again, I wouldn't have gained the broad perspectives that enabled me to start posting regularly on social media; and without writing my LinkedIn articles, I wouldn't be writing this book today! Great opportunities come at inconvenient times.

06

Interests That Could Make Your Job More Bearable

Even your dream job can be unpleasant at times. Unreasonable bosses, nasty teammates and office politics can wear you down. Some jobs involve mundane, repetitive work; others come with plenty of brain-draining administrative duties. It's tempting to quit when you can no longer tolerate that manager who has a habit of adding just a "?" at the top of emails before forwarding them, or when your toxic colleagues try to steal your clients and take credit for your achievements.

But even if you leave your company, there's no guarantee that the people at the next firm will be nicer, and that the boring parts of your old job will be replaced by interesting new tasks. If you're feeling down about your role, I'd advise you to stay put, and see if your mood changes in three to six months. When we're unhappy, we don't make rational decisions because we tend to compare the negative aspects of our current position with the upsides that a new one may bring.

You can also take proactive steps to improve your situation at work. One of the best ways of doing this is by integrating your interests into your role to make it more enjoyable. We all like doing different things, so I can't offer a definitive list of activities that will improve your working life. But based on my own experience, I've made seven suggestions that I hope will spur you to think about how you could incorporate some of your own interests into your job.

Teaching

Running seminars to teach your colleagues new skills builds goodwill and trust, which creates a platform for future collaboration. The workplace provides a great forum to start teaching because you already have a captive audience and a space to hold the event, and your manager is likely to be happy for you to share your knowledge. There's no need to wait until you're asked to teach; check with teammates who might be keen to learn about your area of expertise. Start with a small group, if you're new to teaching.

Food

If you're a foodie, you could take advantage of your job to broaden your culinary experiences. When you eat out with your colleagues, explore new restaurants and different cuisines, or bring them to your new-found favorite restaurants. My work requires traveling to Asian cities, and I often ask my hosts to take me to street food stalls where I can try tasty and authentic local food. I learn about a city's food culture while doing business and building relationships.

Networking

Your work provides the perfect platform to meet new people. But don't just wait until opportunities arise; be proactive and run your own events for colleagues and clients. You could, for example, organize networking drinks or lunches that bring together people from different backgrounds. The exchange of ideas during networking events helps open up new opportunities for you and all who attend. You could introduce colleagues to friends; young professionals to experienced executives; or online LinkedIn connections to offline acquaintances.

Creative Work

I've always enjoyed being creative, so I try to incorporate creativity into my job whenever possible. When I was a junior and had to produce slide decks for clients, I designed them using Apple Keynote (a great alternative to PowerPoint) and made presentations on my MacBook Pro instead of a standard company laptop. At a time when Macs weren't common, I wowed clients with my creative designs and animations, and helped my firm win deals and build relationships in the process. Look out for new trends. If audio-only social networking apps become more popular, for example, you could host events on these platforms to give your colleagues and clients a new experience. Be creative and keep your eyes on the next big thing.

Videography/Photography

Almost everyone owns a smartphone with a good camera, so we can all become budding videographers and photographers. Why not volunteer to take photos and videos at company or client events? You get to practice your skills on free models (i.e. your colleagues), while they get some good (hopefully) videos and photos.

Exercise

If you like exercising and also travel regularly for work, you could combine these two aspects of your life: each time you visit a city, go for a run to explore interesting areas. It's an efficient way to see the sights and keep yourself fit during business trips. I sometimes invite overseas clients to join me for a run instead of a meal. When I was in Sydney visiting clients, my colleague and I went for a lunchtime swim. But you don't need to travel to incorporate exercise into your job. Some people like to take part in group exercises — from dragonboat racing to marathons — with their local colleagues.

Writing

Alongside teaching, writing is another knowledge-sharing activity that you can align with your job. You could write an article about a particular field of technical expertise and post it on LinkedIn, or even get it published in an industry website or magazine. Soon you'll become known, in your company and beyond, as an expert in this area. I know of some law firms that encourage their lawyers to be more active on LinkedIn, so the firms gain visibility with clients and hopefully generate more business. My own writing has developed over time — from publishing in a trade journal during my early career, to posting regularly on LinkedIn today. I struggled with writing at first, but then it became an interest.

I hope you can incorporate some interests into your work, ideally early on into a new role. Your workplace interests will help you build relationships with colleagues. They will also help you get through the tough times and do those mundane tasks because you'll have something to look forward to and energize you.

Part Two

How Social Media and Personal Branding Will Kickstart Your Career

07

What's Your Signature Dish?

Every good restaurant has a signature dish or two. A signature dish makes customers keep coming back, and it's the thing they talk about when they recommend a restaurant to their friends.

When I'm in Hong Kong, I often entertain clients at L'Atelier de Joël Robuchon — it's one of my go-to places there. The late Joël Robuchon was a legendary French chef and restaurateur, who held 32 Michelin stars in 2016. His restaurants have many well-known signature dishes, including a caviar starter featuring 72 evenly spaced dots of cauliflower cream. But the one that gets the most attention is his mashed potato. Robuchon combines ice-cold butter and hot potato at a 1:2 ratio. After vigorous mixing, the result is a fluffy and silky smooth dish. Guess how much it costs? It's free: if you order a main course, you get the mashed potato at no additional charge.

Of course, Robuchon isn't giving away mash and getting nothing in return. "I owe everything to these mashed potatoes," he once said during a demonstration of how to make his most iconic dish. The signature mash offers customers a little bit of nostalgia. It helps turn first-time diners into regular patrons, who spread the word about the great food and encourage more people to visit. The free mashed potato is also an effective marketing tool to attract customers because it appeals to most people's tastes.

But what's one of the most profitable items on Robuchon's menu? It's wine, or more specifically, red wine. There are several benefits that come with red wine: dozens of bottles can be easily stored, the restaurant isn't worried about a rival copying the recipe, and it takes just a minute or so to serve as it requires no preparation.

These red wine and signature dish examples don't just apply to the restaurant trade; we can learn from them and apply them to our careers. The skills you learn at school and in the workplace are mostly red wine skills. They're the core abilities you need to perform the fundamentals of your day job — skills that you and your employer can access as easily as a waiter can pluck a bottle of red wine from the rack. In banking and consulting, red wine skills for junior roles might include financial modeling or pitch-book preparation. In computer engineering, a red wine skill is knowing how to develop an app.

But although red wine skills allow you to do your job well, they're not sufficient to help you advance your career because everyone else in your team has them too. That's why you also need signature skills (your own version of Robuchon's mashed potato) to attract new opportunities and make new contacts. These skills need not be expensive to acquire. Perhaps you could help your colleagues create brilliant social media content or make training videos, for example.

I've had a few signature skills at different stages of my career, so I've learned the importance of not letting them stagnate. Back in the mid-1990s, I worked in foreign exchange (FX) sales at an Asian bank in Singapore. My FX knowledge generated revenues for the bank just like red wine makes money for a restaurant. My mashed potato was my computer programming skills because in those days not many front-office staff knew much about coding. I was able to program FX swap pricing using the C++ language I'd learned as an engineering student. While the bank didn't pay me extra for this, it did get me noticed as a junior. My bosses wanted to automate processes within the department, so they came to me.

When I moved to a regional bank, my risk management skills were the key part of my role: they were my red wine. I also started contributing to financial publications. An article I wrote about bank capital even won me a cash prize from the head of global markets. Publishing technical articles became my new mashed potato. Again, this raised my internal profile because senior managers got to know about me from reading my content in trade journals.

I was at an American bank for most of the 2000s and I took on two new signature skills: photography and running training sessions. I initially covered Asia from the firm's Singapore office, and my seniors across the region — from China to Thailand — often invited me to train staff and clients, and take photos at client offsite events. This helped to strengthen my relationships with several country sales heads in the region.

In 2005, the bank wanted to relocate me to Hong Kong, but I preferred mainland China because the finance sector was opening up there. Fortunately, I now knew the head of China sales quite well through my training courses, so I called him up and asked, "Paulus, I've helped out with training and photos, can I come and work for you?" He readily agreed, and I relocated to Shanghai to set up the derivatives structuring business, where I enjoyed one of the most exciting times of my career, witnessing the liberalization of China's financial sector and the unpegging of the renminbi from the dollar. It wasn't just my (red wine) derivatives skills that got me the job; it was also my version of Robuchon's mashed potato.

A signature skill should be in an area that interests you, so it's easy to acquire and can benefit your colleagues, clients and friends. It should also be unique within your company. Had I worked in a tech firm instead of a bank, my C++ expertise couldn't have been a signature skill because many of my colleagues would have also known the language.

Similar to Robuchon's mashed potato, your signature skill can be a small one that is simple and quick to acquire. It should be useful to a wide range of people including senior managers. As new social media or social networking apps become popular, you could learn about their algorithms, and help friends and colleagues navigate them. Senior managers who are curious about these apps will then go to you for advice.

But remember that when many people around you have acquired the skill, it will no longer be a signature skill of yours, so you'll need to move on to the next one. Keep looking out for new trends ... one of them could well be your next mashed potato.

08
Orange

Toward the beginning of my career I was attending an event and I was introduced to Martin, the owner of a small real estate agency, for the third time in three years. But he had absolutely no idea that he'd met me before. Martin paid little attention to me even after this latest introduction. He seemed to have a condescending attitude to people who didn't come from an elite background.

While I didn't like his attitude, I don't blame Martin for not remembering me because most people have more important things to worry about than remembering a lot of names and faces. Why should he pay attention to someone like me, with my unremarkable face and average build? I was a junior bank employee with neither a big network nor net worth.

And it wasn't just Martin. At school and during the early part of my working life, I tended to remember people, but people didn't remember me. That began to change after I started to dress in the same colors almost every day: I wore a white shirt and a blue suit to work. At first this small action wasn't a ploy to become more noticeable — I did it out of sheer convenience — but over time my consistent dress code made it easier for people to remember me.

A few years ago, when I had just moved from Hong Kong back to Singapore, I often caught up with friends, clients and ex-colleagues in a stand-alone cafe overlooked by the high-rises of Raffles Place in the central business district. On my first visit, I spoke briefly with the manager, Daryl, about how nice the cafe is: customers can see the surrounding greenery and offices through glass walls that make up three sides of the building. When I returned a week later, Daryl greeted me with "Hey Eric!", and I was pleasantly surprised he could recall my name. Our brief previous chat would have helped, but Daryl talks to hundreds of customers every day. More likely, his memory was jogged because I was wearing my standard blue suit and white shirt on both occasions.

I now think of my suit/shirt combination as part of my personal brand — so much so that people are shocked on the rare occasions they see me wearing something different. I once bumped into a former colleague of mine, and one minute into our conversation he asked, "Where's your blue suit today?" This made me realize that we need to be consistent to build a personal brand that will get us recognized. You can't rely on people to remember you, especially in networking events where everyone is trying to meet as many people as they possibly can. You need to help others remember you. So be different ... but in the same way!

Wearing a unique item (such as an eye-catching accessory for women, or a stand-out tie for men) can help add to your brand and make you more recognizable at an event. I've always liked the color orange and over time it's become a consistent part of my personal brand. A few years ago, I wanted to wear something orange with my suit to a networking event, so I sought the help of my former colleague James, who is an art promoter and a very creative man as well as a senior sector banker. He used his own sewing machine to make me a pocket square that was solid orange on one side and featured a Mondrian design (blocks of primary colors) on the other.

This is far from the only orange item that has been made for me. My company, the Institute of Life, has an orange logo, and I carry striking orange business cards in my cardholder. I used to order dozens of orange-colored Pilot ballpoint pens with my email address printed on them, which I gave to clients if they forget to bring their pens to meetings.

Achieving consistency in your personal brand extends well beyond the visual elements. For example, it can be about the content you're associated with. For the past few years I've given talks on career and life skills on a regular basis across a number of locations — from Bangalore to Beijing to Bahrain — as well as online. I shy away from talking solely about investment banking, although there is demand for me to do so. Being a speaker talking about career and life skills is now part of who I am because

I've been consistent in doing this type of work. I'm pretty extreme when it comes to consistency. I stay in the same hotel chain whenever I travel, and buy cars from the same brand no matter which city I'm living in.

Building a strong and consistent personal brand will help people know who you are and what you really stand for. But it's not just about clothes, colors, or the content you like to talk about. Just as we must brand ourselves well offline, we must also do so online, particularly on social media — and that's what I'm going to discuss in the Chapters 9 and 10.

Scan the QR code below or go to https://iol.life/smallactions-ch08/ to see the Mondrain-inspired orange pocket square.

09

The Social Media Platform for Your Self-Development

Before you read the rest of this chapter, I'd like you to Google or Baidu your name alongside your company or university name. For example, I'd search for "Eric Sim Institute of Life". What do you see toward the top of the first page of the search results? I bet it's your LinkedIn profile. My own profile is the first result on Google.

This is a simple exercise, but it shows how important your LinkedIn profile is, even if you're not very active on the platform yet. People that could play a significant role in shaping your career — including hiring managers, HR professionals, colleagues and clients — will form immediate opinions about you based on your profile, and that's before they even meet you in person.

You should think about your LinkedIn profile as more than an online CV that's only useful when you're job hunting. LinkedIn is also an invaluable tool for self-development. It builds your personal brand to include your interests outside of work, and expands your network beyond your company. Let me give you three examples, from two experienced professionals and a student, that illustrate the power of LinkedIn.

Bill's Genuine Interest

I got to know Bill, a mid-ranking finance professional, through an ex-colleague of mine. He'd graduated top of his class, but when I met him he'd been working for a small local asset management company for seven years. Bill wanted to get ahead in life and asked me for some advice. He also told me he enjoyed coaching and was already producing YouTube videos to help university students, but these hadn't gained much traction. I suggested that he post his videos on LinkedIn because his career- and finance-focused content would be more relevant to that platform's professional users.

Bill was a bit skeptical to begin with, but he updated his LinkedIn headline and 'about' section to show his interest in coaching university students. He then started regularly publishing his own content, and engaging with relevant posts from other people. Bill also added appealing images to all his posts. Within just a month, the career services team at a university in Hong Kong found Bill on LinkedIn and invited him to be a career consultant to its students.

But the LinkedIn effect didn't end there for Bill. About a year later, he told me he'd secured a job with a tier-one international bank as a portfolio manager. He said being a career coach to others had got him his ideal role. I was puzzled, so he explained things further. The hiring manager at Bill's new bank wanted someone who could train juniors, and his recent work at the university provided clear evidence that he liked coaching. Bill reckoned other candidates for the job were probably more experienced as portfolio managers and came from bigger financial institutions, but none could show a genuine interest in training young people. Bill's decision to post about coaching via LinkedIn ultimately landed him the position.

Showcase your side interest to differentiate yourself and stand out.

Melissa's Key Skills and Keywords

After reading a few of my articles, Melissa, one of my LinkedIn followers, began to understand the power of LinkedIn. She had worked in corporate strategy and tech for several years, but was hoping to become a management consultant. She used LinkedIn to research the skills that management consulting firms look for, and went on to develop them. As she acquired new skills, she added them to her LinkedIn "about" section. Within a year, HR people at a top global consulting firm were sourcing suitable candidates using a keywords search on LinkedIn. They found Melissa and invited her for an interview. She was soon offered the job of her dreams and has since started work.

Know the key skills and keywords your target audience is looking for, and then develop yourself accordingly.

Ding Becomes a Bridge Builder

I'd also like to tell you about Ding, a university student. Born in China, Ding moved to Singapore aged 16. He really struggled with English when he arrived in the country, and while he gradually got better, he still wasn't confident in his English abilities when I first spoke to him after he attended one of my university lectures. I encouraged Ding to take the plunge and write a LinkedIn article on a topic that played to his strengths, one of which is his understanding of China. Ding then published "9 Things You Must Know When Doing Business in China", which contains some great practical tips — from the best mainland payments apps, to the unwritten rules governing seating arrangements during business lunches and dinners. Despite the high quality of the article, Ding was disappointed because it didn't initially generate much engagement.

I told Ding to persevere and become known on LinkedIn as someone who could make connections between China and Singapore. A few months later, his university got to know about the article and interviewed him about his background and career ambitions for a newsletter that appeared on its website. Ding had gone from a shy young man, who wasn't confident in English, to a student who'd been recognized by his university. Posting that first LinkedIn article was a small action, but it really boosted his confidence. Ding now has a great opportunity to keep using LinkedIn to his advantage, so when he enters the workforce he has further established his unique brand as a bridge builder between Singapore and China.

Ding, Melissa and Bill are just three people among thousands who decided to leverage the power of LinkedIn and experienced big changes in their lives as a result. All three were at first quite reluctant to put themselves out there on LinkedIn, but now they have no regrets because (like me) they have seen what LinkedIn is really capable of.

I hope you'll also be able to use LinkedIn to its full potential. That's why I've dedicated Chapters 10–12 in this section to advising you how to make the most out of social media, including technical tips for writing effective LinkedIn profiles and posts.

10
Consistency

Your internal brand is essentially what people in your company think about you, but it's usually set in stone within your first year on the job. Whether your colleagues initially view you as resourceful, creative, ineffective or useless; it's difficult to change their minds once you become a longer-term employee. While there's little you can do in your day job to boost your internal brand, it's still possible to shift internal perceptions by changing your *external* brand through the strategic use of social media, in particular LinkedIn.

My boss and I once attended a meeting with an important client in China whose company was planning to list shares on the stock exchange. My manager knew the client respected university lecturers, so he introduced me as "Professor Sim". The client laughed at first because he didn't think a senior banker would have the time and inclination to teach, but my boss then asked me to give the client my university business card. I was surprised that he even remembered my second job as a teacher because he was so busy chasing banking deals, but it was at the top of his mind when he introduced me. This goes to show that your outside activities, which you can promote via LinkedIn or other social media, can influence your internal standing.

As we saw in Chapter 9, LinkedIn is a powerful tool that can change the course of your career, so it's perfect for building both your external and internal brands. For example, if you've given a successful speech outside of work, you could post about it on LinkedIn to grow your brand externally.

Then your colleagues who follow you on LinkedIn will know about your talk, which gives your internal brand a nice boost.

But don't just have a LinkedIn strategy; have a social media strategy. Below are three small actions you can take to improve how you approach social media as a professional.

Strategy 1: Use LinkedIn as Your Engine to Drive Other Channels

Think of LinkedIn as the powerful engine that drives your branding on social media. LinkedIn allows you to write longer, more thought-provoking pieces that can get your brand more recognition over time. So when you've developed a topic that will interest your followers, post about it on LinkedIn first. After LinkedIn, you can tweak the post and share it across other relevant social accounts. You can sometimes also share your LinkedIn post with friends via messaging apps. Job and business opportunities can potentially come from any platform.

I became a lecturer at a Hong Kong university in 2016 because an ex-colleague from a U.S. bank saw my Facebook post about a talk I'd given at Cambridge University. She contacted me on behalf of her professor friend, who was looking for a finance professional who knew how to teach. I then met the professor for coffee, and next thing I knew I was made an adjunct associate professor to teach finance and communications.

Strategy 2: Make Your Profile Consistent Across All Platforms

I've already discussed the importance of having a consistent personal brand in your offline life. You should also be consistent when setting up your social profiles. Some of you might have a formal headshot photo for your LinkedIn profile, and use a more casual profile image for Instagram. While that's a popular approach, if you really want to build your brand quickly by making it easily identifiable and consistent, I'd recommend using the same high-quality professional photo for all your channels.

I also use the same title, "banker, lecturer, speaker, writer", across my profiles on LinkedIn, Instagram, Clubhouse, Facebook, Twitter, Telegram, WeChat and WhatsApp. If conversations start on LinkedIn and then move to Telegram, for example, my new connections experience a seamless transition without wondering whether they're still talking to the same person.

Another good reason to stay consistent is because the line between casual and professional relationships is becoming blurred, so many of your connections will see you on several platforms. Your Instagram friend may become your colleague or even your boss one day, and your client or manager may eventually become your Instagram follower. Meanwhile, HR people and hiring managers may try to check all your profiles, not just LinkedIn, before interviewing you, and you should give them a consistent impression.

Strategy 3: Speak the Native Language of Each Platform

While it's important to keep your social profiles consistent, you need to tweak the content of your posts according to the native language of each platform. Here's how I adapt my posting style on some of the main social networks.

LinkedIn

Chapters 11 and 12 are devoted to LinkedIn, but in brief: you should use professional language, add value to readers, and tell a good story. Writing either long articles or short posts is fine, and it's usually best to include a relevant image alongside your text.

Facebook

If a topic has performed well on LinkedIn and is also relevant to my Facebook friends, I may post it on Facebook. I don't publish anything too technical on Facebook. It's best to shorten the post and use a more personal and casual tone.

Instagram

Your text should be even shorter on Instagram (one or two sentences is usually enough) because the photos are the focus. When my LinkedIn posts have powerful pictures that deserve to go on Instagram, I try to do so. When I spoke at a Chartered Financial Analyst (CFA) Institute event in Bahrain, I posted some fun photos of my trip on Instagram alongside some quick tips ("try the local food, visit the national museum") on how to engage with an audience in a new country. My LinkedIn post about the same CFA talk was much longer and more formal, so I respected the native languages of both platforms.

11

How to Write Well on Social Media

When I was 14, I failed an important English literature exam at my high school. I scored just 28 out of 100, a result that really dented my confidence in my writing abilities. Years later, even after doing well at university, I still thought of myself as a poor writer. Despite this lack of confidence, I'd always wanted to write a blog, but I didn't know how to start. I asked a food-blogger friend of mine for some advice, but rather than offering encouraging tips, she just told me to, "use WordPress", and hinted that I was unlikely to make it as a writer.

I could see why she thought that. While I'm a foodie at heart, if I'd tried to write a food blog it might have been too restrictive because I don't eat animal organs, caviar and many raw foods. If I'd blogged about fashion, my readers would have quickly tired of hearing about my white shirts and blue suits. A few friends suggested that I focus on my core expertise (finance and investments), but that might have conflicted with my banking job at the time. Anyway, I still had no clue what WordPress was, and I put my blogging ambitions on hold for a while.

Fortunately, my interest in publishing my ideas online never completely went away. In 2015, I had some time on my hands during the Chinese New Year holiday in Hong Kong, so I convinced myself to post my first LinkedIn article. It took me three days to think about what to write because I kept asking myself, "what's there to share that's not already out there on social media"? After I finally drafted the article, doubts about my own abilities in English made me edit it again and again. As I mustered the courage to click the "post" button on LinkedIn, I worried how my connections (about 300 of them at that time) would view me. Would they laugh at me?

My LinkedIn post was titled "I failed my mathematics exam" (yes, I failed math the year before I failed English). I got about 100 views and seven likes for my very first article on social media. I was overjoyed because when I was in school, my essays usually had only two views: one from my teacher and the other from me. Neither of us liked what we read!

In the past few years, as my articles received more views and likes, things have begun to change. My American friend, Diana, who worked for many years in a senior role in a major financial newspaper, recently complimented me for my excellent writing. Despite receiving this kind of praise from time to time, the 14-year-old boy who failed his literature exam still haunts me today, but he also motivates me to keep improving how I communicate to my followers on LinkedIn. After writing on the platform for more than six years, I've realized that social media readers care about your content more than your language skills, so if English isn't your forte or your first language, don't let that stand in your way.

If you want to have a go at writing, you could contribute articles to trade publications in your industry, but publishing on social media is easier and can help you reach a wider audience. You could start on LinkedIn or choose any other channel that suits your needs. No matter the platform, if you become your own publisher, you get to decide what and when to publish. Here are my top five tips for producing interesting social media content, based on my successes (and failures) on LinkedIn since I started out.

Tell a Personal Story With Universal Application

Our brains are wired to be attracted by stories, so you should tell stories in your social media posts. Whether they're Cinderella-style fables or Mission Impossible movies, stories all have these three core elements: (1) setting, (2) conflict, and (3) resolution. But stories need not be long. The shortest one, generally attributed to American author Ernest Hemingway, has only six words: "For sale: baby shoes, never worn". Personal stories, with universal relevance to the lives of your connections, usually perform well on social media. It's your story, so nobody can say if it's right or wrong.

Always Add Value to Readers

Being upgraded to business or first class on a flight may make you feel euphoric, but writing a post about it doesn't do much for your followers. To build your brand, you should always add value to them and not just post about the basic facts of an event. If you want to write about the great food you just ate, go behind the scenes, talk to the chef, and take photos of the kitchen. If you want to post about your trip overseas, mention a local friend you met while away and tell people what you chatted about.

Start Your Social Posts Strongly

According to a study attributed to Microsoft,[1] the average adult attention span was 12 seconds before the social media age, but by 2015 it had fallen to just eight seconds — shorter than that of a goldfish. You should capture readers' attention with your first sentence. I once wrote two LinkedIn articles about a Singapore street food vendor who won a Michelin star, and posted them a day apart with similar content, except for the first sentence. Which introduction do you prefer?

> "Congratulations to Mr Chan Hon Meng, who was awarded one Michelin star for his chicken noodles …"
> or
> "For 30 years, he's worked 100 hours a week; in the last eight years, he's been selling chicken noodles for less than US$2 a plate."

The first post gathered some 700 likes, which is a lot by LinkedIn standards. But the second one attracted more than 90,000. That just shows the power of starting your post with a bang.

---

[1] https://time.com/3858309/attention-spans-goldfish/

Use Dialogue

Try to use dialogue within stories to bring events to life and pull the reader into your world. The conversations I include in my stories tend to be about everyday situations. Several of my LinkedIn readers have told me that dialogue helps them visualize the settings or scenarios I'm describing. In the following example from LinkedIn, I used dialogue to illustrate how impressed I was with the service at a hotel in Hong Kong.

As I walked into the hotel's grand club lounge, and before I sat down, the service person asked:

"Red wine?"
"Yes," I replied, pleasantly surprised.
"Shiraz?"
"Wow! You remember my order from yesterday!"

I then described the cheerfulness and the willing-to-go-the-extra-mile attitude of Warren, who had recently come to Hong Kong from Mauritius to work in the hospitality industry. But my readers could already see that for themselves because they'd been drawn into our conversation.

Do Interesting Things Offline

It's difficult to post original and engaging stories and images, if you're not doing anything interesting in your offline life. Only by constantly trying new things can you have new experiences and perspectives to share with your social media audience. In recent years, I've spoken to small shop owners to seek out their stories, attended videography classes, and tried out audio-chat apps when they were still in their beta versions. You should choose your own new adventures and create your content around them.

Producing content for social media still isn't always straightforward for me, but I've learned many lessons. In Chapter 12 I'll explain how to build your following on LinkedIn.

12

Secrets to Attracting More Followers

In 2020, I made two of LinkedIn's lists for its content creators: China Spotlight and Singapore Top Voices. It's such an honor that my LinkedIn work has been recognized for driving thoughtful and professional conversations.

I'm sometimes asked to reveal my secrets on increasing engagement and number of followers on LinkedIn. My initial advice is that the quality of your followers is more important than the quantity. And the quality of your content is the foundation for building your follower base. But while you focus on producing quality content, there are other things you can do to help you become more widely followed on LinkedIn. Here are my seven tips.

Comment on Other People's Posts

When I come across an interesting LinkedIn post, I try to leave an insightful comment, which often prompts the author to engage with me. With engagement comes more visibility. If your comments add value to readers, they will follow you. Commenting takes only a few minutes, so it's an efficient way to add value to readers.

Reveal Failure

Most social media posts only show the positive side of life, but we all know that life has its ups and downs. When you publish something that exposes your weaknesses, you make it easier for people to identify with you and to share their own failures. You help take the pressure off people to be perfect all the time. Revealing failures makes the stories you tell on LinkedIn more interesting (remember that when there's no conflict, there's no story) and makes you more likable. This phenomenon is known as the Pratfall effect. It was discovered in 1966 by social psychologist Elliot Aronson, who demonstrated that highly competent people are perceived as more likable when they perform an ordinary blunder.

Be Observant

To attract followers on LinkedIn, you need to have interesting and fresh ideas on a regular basis. Some people ask me how I develop such a wide range of topics to write about and yet still stay within the general theme of career and life skills. The answer: I observe my surroundings and the people I encounter. When I find a potential topic for a LinkedIn article, I immediately note it down on my phone. My article ideas often come from people in everyday life, including my tailor in Hong Kong, a tour guide in London, and gardeners tending to lotus plants at Gardens by the Bay in Singapore. Sometimes I simply go out to my own garden and learn from nature. If you engage with people and your environment, you can learn lessons from them and translate those lessons into appealing content that adds value to your followers.

Speak at Events

I get invited to speak at events almost every month. On the final slide of my presentations, I share my social media usernames in case attendees want to follow me. I also post a summary of my speech on LinkedIn. I usually see an uptick in my follower numbers after each talk. If you don't have the opportunity to present at events yet, try to arrange speaking sessions at your university or workplace to share your hobbies, specialist skills or topics you're interested in.

SEO Your LinkedIn Profile

Ahead of each speaking event, the organizers usually ask me for my biography to post on their website, and I make sure to include my LinkedIn URL (www.linkedin.com/in/simeric) in the bio. Over the years, my LinkedIn profile page has been backlinked like this on the websites of many organizations, including those of top universities, whose sites typically have a high domain authority. Search engine algorithms figure out that these links all point back to my LinkedIn, and this helps with the search engine optimization (SEO) of my profile, so it appears higher up the results page when people search for my name.

Network Offline

It's a good idea to network to add value over and above just posting content. This will keep your followers happy and help you attract new ones. For example, I organize online and offline networking events for some of my followers who regularly engage with my posts. I'm curious to know who they are and why they enjoy my content. Shakiru, a crude oil trading analyst based in London, liked my very first LinkedIn article, "I failed my mathematics exam". At that time, I had just a few hundred connections. Whenever I visit London, I always invite Shakiru to join my networking events and introduce him to my other London-based friends and connections. Meeting face to face helps strengthen our relationship.

Be Like Bamboo

A journalist writing for a tech magazine asked me whether the increase in my LinkedIn followers resembled a linear or exponential pattern. It was the latter. At the beginning, I made slow progress in gaining followers, but I still enjoyed writing my articles. Users like Shakiru, through engaging with my posts, helped me to build a foundation of followers, improve my writing, and expand my thinking. This is just like how bamboo grows. When I planted some bamboo in my garden, nothing much happened in the first year, then new bamboo suddenly shot up by a few metres within weeks.

A blog of a million followers starts with a single connection.

Part Three

Build Social Capital and Expand Your Network

What is Social Capital?

The first part of my career was quite good, but nothing to really shout about. Then one day an ex-colleague called to ask me if I was keen to move. His boss was looking for someone with my skill set. Of course I was keen: it was the job of my dreams at one of the most recognized financial institutions in the world. I got the role, and had opportunities to work across various functions in Singapore, Shanghai and Hong Kong during my eight years at the firm. From this time onward, none of my new positions — whether as a banker or teacher — came about by me answering an advertisement. All were the result of being recommended by people in my network.

I attribute my good fortune to the social capital I've accumulated over the years with people I know. Social capital is the good will that you gradually build up with others. It works a bit like depositing money in a bank and seeing your savings grow. Each time you're nice to someone or help them, you generate some social capital.

Social capital is also important if you decide to start your own business later on in your career. Your first 50 customers are likely to buy from you based on the social capital you've accumulated with them. My ex-colleague, Louis, was supportive of me during the time we worked together. Several years later, he told me his wife had started a tea delivery business. I immediately bought a box of premium Chinese tea to help them test their online ordering and payment system. I hope they're off to a good start.

How can you begin to create some social capital? You should be generous to others, treat them with respect, and assume they're going to do much better in life in the future. A small action like buying a colleague lunch adds to your social capital, as does making an extra effort to help a client solve a problem outside of your job scope.

Don't expect the same people you've helped to return all your favors, and don't expect to benefit in the near term. Have a horizon of 10, 15, or even 20 years. In the long run, many people will recognize the kindness you've shown them, and this will open doors for you that would otherwise have been closed. Without social capital, you might not even know these doors were even there.

13

Know Your Restaurants Well

I was sitting in the opulent and intimate surroundings of Fook Lam Moon, a Cantonese restaurant in Hong Kong's Wan Chai district that was first opened in 1948 and is often called the "cafeteria for the wealthy". I was there with my colleague KK, who headed up Hong Kong sales and trading for my bank, and we were sipping Chinese tea and waiting for our clients to meet us for lunch.

Suddenly KK's mobile phone rang. It was the manager of another restaurant, the Forum, a Michelin-starred establishment that's renowned for its abalone. The manager knew KK well and was calling to say that his clients had arrived. This naturally confused KK as he hadn't made a reservation at Forum. He soon realized that our clients had gone to the incorrect restaurant! Forum is pronounced "Foo Lam" in Cantonese, so it sounds similar to Fook Lam Moon. We left the "right" restaurant and rushed over to the "wrong" one. Luckily, it was only a nine-minute taxi ride away in Causeway Bay.

I was impressed by how the manager at Forum had handled the situation. When the clients had turned up, he had politely shown them to a table without telling them there was no booking under the name KK. The manager had assumed that KK had forgotten to make a reservation and he didn't want to embarrass my senior colleague by mentioning this to the clients. He'd had KK's number so was able to call him as soon as the guests were seated. Why had the manager gone out of his way to keep both KK and his clients happy? It was because KK had such a strong relationship with him, built up over several years of him frequenting the Forum Restaurant.

When KK and I made it to Forum, our lunch got off to a good start as we all laughed about the clients' confusion and how the manager had saved the day. This experience made me realize how important it is to really get to know our favorite restaurants. I saw how superb KK is at building and maintaining relationships with people — be they clients, colleagues … or restaurant managers.

A New Sushi Experience

I soon began to emulate KK and would dine at a restaurant a few times a month to get to know the chef, manager and waiting staff. One weekend when I was out with my family I stumbled across Tomokazu, a Japanese restaurant not far from the Forum in Hong Kong. Tomokazu serves the most delicious sushi I've ever tasted and some of its fish are flown in daily from Japan. I chatted to the sushi chef on my first and second visits, so when I came back again he knew my taste and I didn't have to order from the menu. I prefer a mixture of aburi (which is seared with a blow torch) and raw sushi. Tomokazu's chef always starts my meals with a salad, before serving a few pieces of raw sushi, and then the seared fish, one plate at a time.

Knowing this restaurant well enabled me to build social capital with colleagues and friends by making them feel special and offering them new experiences. I invited a vegetarian colleague from India to dine with me at Tomokazu. I messaged the chef to ask whether he would make some vegetable sushi. He said, "sure, no problem!", and he did a beautiful job preparing the food. My colleague hadn't tried much sushi before, but he instantly became a fan.

A week later, I took a friend to the same restaurant and asked him to order by pointing at the fish on display. When he did so, the chef said, "For Mr Sim's friends, we have an even better one." The chef then took a slab of ultra-high-grade fish from the fridge below the sushi counter. My friend was delighted to say the least. Knowing the chef certainly has its benefits!

Local Food for the Foreign CFO

You can sometimes cater to the culinary tastes of your colleagues, friends and clients without taking them to up-scale places like Tomokazu and Forum. One of my clients, the CFO of a large international real estate company, was visiting Singapore from Tokyo. I flew in from Hong Kong to meet him for dinner. I guessed that he'd been to many fancy restaurants in Singapore already, and I knew from our previous correspondence that he wanted to try local eateries. I brought him to a roadside seafood stall that I know well — it doesn't have air conditioning, but it does serve wonderful crab vermicelli. My client enjoyed the evening so much that he sent me a letter of thanks from Japan to Hong Kong, which I've summarized below:

> Dear Mr Eric Sim,
>
> I would like to extend my sincere gratitude for your arrangement at the local seafood restaurant during my recent visit to Singapore. Thank you for taking me to wonderful places as always. Your choice of cuisine is always good, and I have enjoyed them all. I hope we can continue and expand our successful business relationship going forward.

I have two or three go-to restaurants in each city that I visit regularly. You can do the same. They don't have to be expensive establishments. The secret is to find small, independent restaurants where it's easy to strike up conversations with the manager, owner or chef. If the place is large and has too many diners, the staff may soon forget you.

You can build rapport with the manager over time. Don't just chat about food; reveal a bit about yourself as you would in any relationship. This helps them remember you and makes it easier for them to talk to you next time you visit. It's also important to become familiar with the restaurant's food, so you can recommend the best items on the menu, and avoid ordering the wrong dishes for your guests. Finally, you should understand your guests' food preferences before you choose which of your favorite places to take them to. I knew the Japanese CFO was adventurous enough to try food outside of posh hotels and fine-dining restaurants, and many of my Indian friends are vegetarians.

Some of us take eating out for granted, especially when it's for work. We invite overseas colleagues or important clients for meals at restaurants we've never tried before because they're in a convenient location, or have a well-designed website, or good online reviews. But when we arrive, the manager doesn't give us the best table, the waiter doesn't welcome us with a smile, we don't know what to order, and the chef won't cook anything off the menu.

If you know the staff and food of a few restaurants really well, your clients or colleagues (or whoever is with you) will enjoy a far better all-round experience. They'll have fond memories of the meal and associate you with their pleasant dining experience. Your relationship with them will blossom, and you'll accumulate social capital.

14

Cultural Curiosity on a Plate

If you do business globally, or if you work for a company with a diverse workforce, having cultural curiosity is one of the keys to your success. Compared with some people I know, who have a vast knowledge of many countries and cultures, I can't say I have a very high level of cultural awareness. But I do have cultural curiosity: when I meet someone from overseas, I'm interested to find out more about their culture.

What's the best way to develop cultural curiosity? Reading books has its advantages, but it isn't collaborative. Moreover, if you study too deeply, you risk stereotyping people according to their nationality alone and overlooking other factors (e.g. their stage of life, gender, and interests) that can also help shape their personalities. When the Clubhouse app was in its beta version, I regularly went on it to listen to what people from other countries had to say. It's an interactive platform that can help you understand foreign cultures a little better, but it can be time consuming.

Another way to develop cultural curiosity is through food. When you try local dishes and ask your hosts questions about them, you open up wider discussions about history and culture. If a visitor to Singapore or Hong Kong talks to me about the tastes and origins of local street food, it instantly makes our conversation interesting. Of course, I'd be naive to think that eating a few local meals will turn anyone into a cultural expert, but it can be a fun way to establish new relationships and build social capital.

Cook's Taste of Asia

During a visit to Asia, Apple CEO Tim Cook made a point of trying various local cuisines … and tweeting about his experiences. In Bangkok, he ate with two food bloggers and sampled some of the city's best street food, including an "amazing" crab omelet. After meeting pop star Gen Hoshino in Japan, Cook tweeted that he loved the *izakaya* bar they'd dined at. When Cook was in Singapore, two iPhone photographers showed him around the historic Tiong Bahru district and took him for breakfast at a local food center. Cook thanked them for sharing their love of the area's "rich heritage" and for ordering "amazing food". Cook's three tweets, which all included pictures of him eating local food, were very popular. Images of the CEO of one of the world's most valuable companies enjoying tasty meals in humble eateries struck a chord with local communities.

Hot Dogs on a Cold Night

It was my first trip to New York, and I landed late in the evening. After checking into my hotel near Grand Central, I went out to look for a nearby hot dog stand. I'd seen people eating New York's famous hot dogs so many times in movies, so now I wanted to try one for myself. The taste of the frankfurter, sauces, fried onion, and soft white bun was unbeatable on a cold spring night. It was one of the most delicious meals of my trip. Thinking about my first proper hot dog reminds me of a quote I read in the book *It Worked for Me: In Life and Leadership* by Colin Powell, the New York-born former United States Secretary of State.

"Hot dog diplomacy may not be earth-moving, but it allows two people to develop a human relationship that will help sustain an official relationship in good times and bad."[1]

Powell is saying that, even in the high-stakes world of international diplomacy, you can start to build social capital with another person via something as simple and universal as street food. I've tried to do this in my own career.

---

[1] Powell, C., & Koltz, T. (2014). *It Worked for Me: In Life and Leadership*. New York: Harper Perennial.

Building Social Capital in India and Bahrain

Before I went to India for the first time, I was advised to drink only bottled water and to avoid eating fruit, salad and yogurt. But the food in New Delhi was so good that when I visited India again a few months later — this time to Bengaluru — I tried many more dishes. The *murgh makhani* (butter chicken) I had during that trip was excellent. I instantly clicked with my hosts when they saw how eager I was to try many different foods. There was much to discuss as I found out more about the different spices and the part they play in Indian culture.

On my first day in Bahrain, I asked a taxi driver to take me to a restaurant to try a typical local meal. He brought me to one and I ordered chicken biryani. The next day, I shared my little adventure with my audience at the start of a speech at a conference. This is what one of the attendees, Mohammed, wrote about my presentation in a LinkedIn post:

> "He started his talk by sharing an interesting and warm experience of his visit to a famous local restaurant on his first day in Bahrain. His story and photos from his visit created an instant and warm connection, and made you tune in to everything else he had to say after that. While this is something a lot of speakers and leaders consciously attempt to do, Eric did it in a very natural, simple, and honest manner."

I didn't plan for this to happen, but it seems my curiosity about Bahrain's food culture helped me connect with the audience, including Mohammed, who also wrote that my talk motivated him to take up writing again after a 15-year break. Chatting about food, whether in a restaurant or to an audience of hundreds, is a wonderful icebreaker. People then listen to you more intently when the conversation moves to other topics because you've already established a rapport with them.

Food Memory

The human tongue has long-term "memory". What you eat (and don't eat) as a child can help determine your taste for the rest of your life. Your preferences can be hard to change, and you pass them onto the next generation. Asking questions about the origins of another country's food deepens your cultural knowledge. You may even find that the talk flows naturally into the history of that nation.

If you go to a Korean restaurant, you'll probably find *nurungji* (scorched rice) on the menu. These days chefs intentionally burn rice to produce the crispy texture and nutty taste of *nurungji*, which is enjoyed on its own or in a soup or tea. But if you ask about the history of the dish, you'll learn that rice was traditionally cooked in pots before modern rice cookers became popular. In less prosperous times, when food was in short supply, it was important to use up every last grain of rice — including any overcooked rice at the bottom of the pot. Cooks would scrape off the scorched rice and serve it up. The tradition of *nurungji* has since been passed from generation to generation. Times have changed and there is no shortage of rice in Korea, but the food memory remains.

Visitors to Singapore, Malaysia and Indonesia are often curious about the Peranakan culture. Peranakans descend from Chinese immigrants who married locals in the region from the 15th century onward. They have a diverse and complex history that covers everything from language to clothing and architecture. While it's impossible to understand Peranakan traditions on a short trip, you can gain some initial insights by trying out their food, which fuses Chinese cuisine with Southeast Asian spices. And if you take a Peranakan food tour of Singapore, you'll discover more about the history of the island.

Showing cultural curiosity through food involves the small actions of eating and talking, but it serves as a platform for getting to know more about a country and its heritage. Food, especially authentic street food that's been made in the same way for generations, embodies the essence of a culture. Eating and sharing good food always puts people in a happy mood, so your willingness to sample local dishes while overseas will also help you build closer relationships with your foreign friends, colleagues and clients. Foreigners don't expect us to understand everything about their culture, but they love it when we enjoy their food.

15

How to Reach Out and Make High-Quality Connections

We typically have three broad types of relationships in our lives: (1) family and friends, (2) acquaintances, and (3) high-quality connections (HQCs).

You need your close friends and family to support you and cheer you up when you're down, and you should be there for them when they need you. But when it comes to your career, this first group may not help you out very much. If you're in your 20s, your best friends may be looking for similar jobs, or working in fields that aren't of any interest to you. Acquaintances are people you know only loosely. Perhaps they're your neighbors or folks you say hi to at your gym. You may be connected to them on social media, but you seldom have in-depth discussions.

By contrast, you can have interesting chats with your high-quality connections. HQCs don't have to be close to you on a personal level — they won't mind if you don't know their birthday — but they can motivate you and help you expand your career horizons. Your HQCs could be senior and successful, but they don't need to be. Instead of focusing on seniority, I try to connect with inspiring people across different industries and countries, who have a passion for life, and skills that compliment mine.

I once received a LinkedIn message out of the blue from a young American named John. He was working in Shanghai for a Chinese securities house after having completed his master's in that city.

"Dear Eric. Hope all is well. I've been following your LinkedIn page for a while now, and you really put out some interesting and informative content. I can really see you're passionate about helping and teaching the younger generation, and as a part of that generation, I appreciate it. I saw you'll be speaking at a digital marketing conference in Shanghai in a few weeks' time …"

John went on to ask if I could meet him for a coffee to give him some career advice. I had to politely turn him down. My schedule in Shanghai was too hectic. But instead of being disheartened that he couldn't meet me one-on-one, John wrote me a sincere reply, thanking me for getting back to him and acknowledging how busy I was. After reading this, I invited John to attend my presentation instead. He grabbed the opportunity and took time off work to see me on stage. When my speech was over, John joined a small group from the audience who were talking to me, so we were introduced to each other after all.

When you want to meet new people, especially sought-after professionals with many demands on their time, be prepared to be rebuffed after you initially contact them — like John was. But if you're rejected, don't give up. If you write a polite follow-up and rearrange your plans to suit the other person, you increase your chances of success.

How did my relationship with John develop from there? He became a teaching assistant of mine from time to time. When I spent a day lecturing at universities in Beijing, Singapore and Hong Kong, John would fly in from Shanghai at his own expense and talk to my students about his experiences as a foreign finance professional working in China. John's speaking slots only lasted a few minutes, so he was going out of his way to maintain me as a high-quality connection. Although I could have asked various other young professionals to address my students, I chose John because of his proactive attitude. His willingness to jump on a plane to be my assistant showed how sincere he was. John later posted the following message (abbreviated for this book) on LinkedIn:

"It's not often that you meet someone who truly changes your life, but on this very day three years ago I met someone who did that. I just want to share a small note of appreciation to Eric Sim for all he's done for me over the years, and for changing my life for the better. From teaching me about personal branding, inspiring me to start writing on LinkedIn, bringing me to lectures at leading universities across Asia, teaching me numerous life lessons, and much more — I can truly say his impact on me has been tremendous. I wouldn't be where I am today if it wasn't for him."

John's persistence paid off. But determination isn't the only important aspect of establishing and maintaining high-quality connections. Here's what else you need to consider.

Offer a Point of Difference

You should target people who may find you unique. For example, if you're a young professional from Europe, don't be afraid to reach out to an experienced professional in Asia. You don't have to be unique in a general sense, you just need to be unique (e.g. by age, geography or skills) to the person you're contacting.

You Don't Need to Meet HQCs in Person

While it's always good to meet in person, I've successfully worked with several HQCs whom I've never seen face to face. Teddy, a website designer based in Vietnam, offered his services to help me build my company website. After his numerous follow-ups, I engaged him and he did a great job. My website is up and running. Geneva-based Lisa has helped me moderate online events numerous times. I've yet to meet either of them in person.

Personalize Your First Message

When you contact someone online for the first time, don't make your message sound like it's been cut and pasted from a template you're using for lots of other people. Tailor your text to the individual, for example by mentioning specific points in their online articles that resonate with you. This increases your chances of getting a response.

Don't Let Rejection Stand in Your Way

You may get rejected or ignored even after you follow up with someone. Don't let that experience put you off contacting other potential HQCs on LinkedIn in the future. You'll likely be rebuffed as much as 90% of the time, so you should persevere to reach the 10% of people who will develop into HQCs. Given my seniority and large online following, you may think that everyone I message wants to work with me, but this isn't the case — sometimes even junior people don't bother replying. Rejection is normal.

Be a Connector

When you've established an HQC, keep these valuable contacts warm. One way of doing this is to be a connector: introduce some of your HQCs to each other. They're likely to do the same for you. Avoid introducing people doing similar jobs, even though that may seem like an obvious option. When I introduce myself as a trainer, my new connections often want to link me up with other trainers, but I'm not so interested because I already have skills and contacts in that sector. You should instead match people with complimentary backgrounds: hiring managers to jobs seekers; students to practitioners.

Use Interesting Articles to Engage With Your HQCs

I've found it helpful to maintain my HQCs by engaging with them via the content they post on LinkedIn. I make sure to read and comment on some of their articles to show that I value their opinions. I also send them direct messages with links to interesting content that I've recently come across. When I attend an online event where an HQC is presenting, I take a screenshot and send it to them.

Making and maintaining HQCs is all about interacting with your connections and offering them something in return. The relationship can't be one way. I'm John's HQC because I can teach him career and life skills. He is an HQC of mine because through him and his friends, I can learn about young people's thinking, interests and priorities.

We grow in our careers and in our lives based on who we engage with — and that's what makes HQCs so important. Fortunately, social media enables us to develop and maintain relationships easily. We can communicate online with people from different countries and industries to enrich ourselves. We can work closely with people we've never (or barely) met in person, but who can motivate us, advise us and give us new skills and knowledge.

16

Juniors Can Add Value Too

James was studying at a business school in Madrid and was also head of events for the school's finance club. He reached out via LinkedIn to invite me to give a talk to the club's members about the key skills required to get a good job. When we had a call to discuss his proposal, James told me that the online event would expand my profile in Europe, and that he'd be happy to connect me with people in his network even after the session was over. I hadn't given any talks in Europe before, so James' pitch was attractive. He also had the right mindset for building a relationship because he was thinking about how he could appeal to me by adding value to me.

But James wasn't taking any chances. He then asked me directly whether there was anything else he could do to ensure the webinar was worth my while. I told him to make the event official so it would benefit more students. He agreed to open it up to the entire university, not just his finance club. He'd invite alumni too, and would find a professor to introduce me before I spoke.

James then sought help from the school's engagement manager, Dylan, who readily agreed to provide marketing and technical support. But getting someone to host the event wasn't so easy. James approached a finance professor and an academic who specializes in Asian markets, but neither were too keen. He persevered and eventually signed up a marketing professor, who was also the school's vice president for talent and careers, to host the event and help me craft my speech.

Dylan thought of a brilliant name to market the webinar, "Careers after Corona", and used LinkedIn Live to attract people. More than 500 current and past students attended on the day, which broke the school's record for an online career event. Attendees gave fantastic feedback. James was delighted that he'd pulled it off.

Three months later, when interviewing for an internship with a top investment bank, James shared how he'd managed to convince me to accept his invitation and persuade his professor to get involved. James had told the professor that the event would raise awareness of the university in Asia and help European students develop a better understanding of the region. That impressed the interviewers and he was offered the coveted internship. Key to his success was his belief that adding value to others is critical to relationship building and getting things done.

We can learn lessons from James. When you approach someone, make sure your new proposal adds value to them, or that you've already added value through a past interaction and have since kept in touch. I really appreciate the efforts of people like James who come to me with ideas that may be beneficial to both of us. My time is limited, so I prioritize people like James, if they want my help in the future. When James asks for career advice, I'm always happy to offer some.

James' story also shows that juniors can still add a lot of value to relationships with senior people. If you're junior, don't underestimate what you can offer. If you're more experienced, don't overlook your younger colleagues.

I was once at a networking event and met a fairly experienced professional named Patricia. I saw her suck up to senior management from her company and ignore the juniors. Smart leaders can tell when you're schmoozing them just because of their job title, and they'll pay attention to how well you treat your subordinates because this says a lot about your character. If you help juniors, they'll speak highly of you, and this feedback will get through to those above you. You'll be more likely to be promoted. Some juniors may be fast tracked for top jobs and could end up becoming your boss in the future. As for Patricia — unfortunately she was sidelined at her firm less than a year after the networking event.

Your career is a long game, and people at all levels can play a part in your success. Try not to be shortsighted. When I worked in banking, I made it a point to train juniors. Even though I've now left my previous banks, many of my former junior colleagues still keep in contact with me. It would have been sad if our relationships had only been based on me being a managing director at their bank.

Whether you're junior or senior, you should stay in touch with people on a regular basis to keep your relationships strong. Avoid reaching out to people only when you need help or have something to sell. And remember to add value to the relationships, so that both parties gain from working together.

17

To Go Fast, Go Alone
To Go Far, Go Together

When my friend EC opened a new boutique gym, I was keen to check it out. As soon as I arrived I was struck by the environment he'd created. Instead of bright lights, mirrors and rows of machines, EC had set up a darkly lit and Spartan exercise room, designed for immersing yourself in high-intensity workout classes as music blares out in the background.

But what really grabbed my attention on that first visit was an inspirational sign, which dominated an entire wall of the gym with its large black characters, outlined in striking neon green. It says: "If you want to go fast, go alone. If you want to go far, go together". After some research, I discovered that this popular proverb is generally thought to have come from the African continent, although its precise origins are unknown. The more I thought about these words, the more they made sense to me. When I want to do ambitious new things that are beyond my current skill set — when I want to "go far" — I try to work together with a partner who can help me reach my goals.

I'm not referring here to bulk standard teamwork within a company. Most organizations promote the importance of being a "team player", and develop their own set of clichéd slogans like "teamwork makes the dream work" and "there is no I in team". But this is often a ruse: we're ultimately competing with people in our teams because they're doing similar jobs to us and want the same promotions as us. Moreover, our teams are largely the result of external recruitment and internal hierarchies that we have little or no control over.

To "go far" and achieve longer-lasting success, we can't rely on our employers to ensure we're working with the right type of people. We should instead take the initiative ourselves and proactively partner with individuals outside our teams — and even outside our organizations — whose skills and strengths complement and are different from our own.

The Partnership That Produced this Book

The book you're now reading is the result of such a partnership. I've been writing career advice on LinkedIn for several years, but I write primarily based on what I'm experiencing at the time. My posts are chronological, which can make searching for articles by topic more difficult. I thought it would be great to structure my content more clearly into different themes, add some new topics, and give people easy access to my ideas in a book. Working alone, I rapidly gained LinkedIn followers. But I realized that if I wanted to go further with my writing and reach even more people by publishing a book, I needed to follow the African proverb and work together with someone. A book requires a lot of effort in terms of planning, turning ideas into words, and fine-tuning the language for a global audience.

I once did a one-day creative writing course, but I didn't learn much! I decided it would be better to partner with a professional writer as my co-author for the book rather than attend more writing classes. This would also enable me to spread my workload because I wanted to continue my teaching, speaking, and social media work. As you can see from the cover of this book, the person I had in mind was Simon Mortlock, an editor and content manager at eFinancialCareers, a careers website for the financial services and technology sectors. I've been collaborating with Simon since he first contacted me for my views as a senior banker several years ago. I write guest articles for his website on topics of interest to his career-minded readers. Our relationship works because our backgrounds and skills are complementary rather than overlapping, so together we bring more to the table. I'm an Asian banker and lecturer, while he's a Western editor and journalist.

Going Further as a Speaker

I've been a teacher and public speaker for many years now, but more recently I've had the privilege of talking to audiences in more places around the world, including New Delhi, Kuala Lumpur, Beijing, Bahrain and London. I've managed to "go far" (literally in this case) with my speaking career thanks to working together with the CFA (Chartered Financial Analyst) Institute. I was based in Hong Kong when staff from the CFA asked me for a meeting at my Institute of Life office in Cyberport, a hub for digital businesses. I then agreed to speak at the CFA Annual Conference. I soon forged a strong partnership with staff and members from the institute and its societies. During the pandemic, we attracted more than 2,500 signups for a webinar. My relationship with the CFA has greatly increased my reach as a speaker. I couldn't have gone this far by myself.

Seek out Partners in Your Organization

Not all your partnerships need to be outside of your company. I tried to have one or two partners in other departments at the firms I worked for — people I could discuss ideas with freely without worrying that we might be competing against each other for our next promotion.

When I was in investment banking in Hong Kong, I worked closely with Elle, who was in the wealth management division. We complemented each other well because we offered clients different skills and product know-how. While I could have focused exclusively on investment banking transactions, to go further in my banking career and expand my knowledge base, I decided to learn about wealth management through Elle. Partnering can be the best way to get to grips with a new field because you typically take on information more effectively working on a real project than you do when studying theory in a classroom. My efforts with Elle paid off. By investing time in this cross-divisional partnership (and not fixating on short-term issues like profit sharing), we closed several deals together. Our partnership also gave me more visibility and credibility within the bank.

While building a partnership like the one with Elle takes time, it all begins with a small action like buying coffee. Simon didn't contact me about writing this book; I reached out to him to broach the idea. Sometimes the best partnerships come about when you instigate them yourself.

At the start of your career you may find that you make fast progress within the comparatively narrow scope of your job. But you won't "go far", and your career will eventually become constrained to just one area of expertise, unless you work together with people whose skills are complementary to yours. When I identify a new area of interest, such as producing high-quality live streaming events, I look out for potential partners. When I find someone with complementary skills, I write down their name in my phone. I also think about what I can bring to the relationship. Working together involves give and take, so both you and your partners can "go far". See if you can create a mini project or fun event that brings different people together.

You don't have to believe in those empty corporate "one team one dream" catchphrases. To expand your career, it's best to partner with a few people inside or outside your company who can help take you in exciting new directions and help you learn new skills.

18

How to Organize Your Own Networking Event

Meeting face-to-face is still important even though networking online can be quite effective with the video conference tools we have at our fingertips. But meeting strangers at events, or finding people to speak with at big gatherings can be daunting to many people, including me. Do you barge into a group that's already chatting? Do you strike up a conversation from scratch with someone standing alone? And even if you do get talking, it's far from certain that the other people will actually be interesting. You may spend most of the evening making up excuses to escape them.

I don't really enjoy going to networking events unless I know the organizer, but I do like hosting my own, primarily because this allows me to bring relationships from online to offline. I usually choose a diverse and dynamic group of attendees, who I know will enjoy mixing with each other and with me.

You can run mini networking events no matter your level. If you're a junior professional, don't just invite your contemporaries. It's likely that one or two senior people will want to attend, so they can meet interesting people from your generation. You can keep costs under control by holding get-togethers at bars, and only paying for the first round of drinks. How should you go about setting up and running a successful networking session? Here are my top tips, based on the many times I've organized these events.

Keep Control of Your Numbers

Resist the temptation to send invites to all and sundry. If more than about 20 people turn up, it becomes harder to talk to everyone in any depth. I think the ideal size is eight to 12 guests, but you can go as low as five and still have a worthwhile evening. Focus not on the quantity of people, but on the ideas and experience that each person brings.

Invite a Diverse Group

When I first started organizing networking drinks, I just invited colleagues from other departments of my bank. I later included people from the wider banking sector. These days I don't limit myself to financial services. I ask a mixed bunch of folks — from tour guides, engineers and lawyers, to designers and videographers — to attend, so we can all meet people with different skills and experience from other industries. To make the evening more engaging for everyone, I also try to ensure my events are diverse in terms of gender, age and nationality. The thing all of my guests have in common is curiosity and an interest in learning new skills.

Allow People to Arrive at Different Times

You don't need to design a fancy invitation to your event. Send messages to your connections and let attendees arrive at different times. If there's someone you want to discuss business with, suggest that they come earlier — at, say, 5.30 pm. If you know junior people will be stuck at their desks that evening, allow them to arrive later than the others. By contrast, older attendees may want to get to the bar as soon as they can, so they can leave early to spend time with their kids. It's not only your guests who'll benefit if you're flexible with timings. Staggered arrivals will allow you to spend quality time with each guest as they turn up.

Take Control of Introductions and Make Them Memorable

Aside from any friends they bring along, I'm usually the only person that my guests will know at my events, so I make a point of introducing them myself. At the start of the evening I do this as each guest arrives, but when the crowd grows larger, I wait until three new people come along. Most people are too humble to make an interesting introduction, and they just mention their names and job titles, which are quickly forgotten by the rest of the group. I like to say something memorable, which will spark up a conversation. Here's an example: "meet Cindy, London's most interesting tour guide. She knows every little shop on Jermyn Street and Savile Row like the back of her hand."

Get Some Food

Networking events can be a bit scary for some, and it can take a while to get people talking. This is even more so in Asia, where people tend to be a bit shy. I always order some food to give my guests something to talk about or do. They can ask, "do you want some nachos?" or, "how are the chicken wings". When I hosted a networking event at my Hong Kong office in Cyberport for students and market practitioners, I ordered some do-it-yourself Singapore spring rolls (*popiah*). Making them served as a fun icebreaker to get my guests to mingle with each other. It was funny to see the end products made by a few of my foreign guests. They looked nothing like the spring rolls I know.

Be a Matchmaker

As a host, make it your job throughout the evening to pull someone from one group to meet another person across the room. If possible, try to bring together people who have complimentary needs: a real estate banker and an architect; a local and a new visitor to the city; a student and a senior executive. Always keep your eyes and ears open. If you see that someone looks bored, talk to them and introduce different people to them.

Post a Photo of Your Networking Event

Be sure to take a good group photo and post it on social media after the event to bring your relationships from offline to online. Posting the image also lets your other friends and contacts see who was there. Some may get in touch to say they know one of the attendees, so you establish a mutual connection. The relationship building continues even after the event ends.

Choose the Same Venue Next Time

If your first networking evening goes well, hold it in the same place next time. When you run your second session, you'll know which part of the bar is most conducive to getting people mingling and talking. Don't choose an area that lets all your guests sit down on a long table. It's better to have a smaller table surrounded by standing space, so attendees can move about freely and talk to different people. Be sure to always treat the waiting staff well, and tip them if you can afford it. This can pay dividends when you return to the venue. I usually plan for about 80% of my invitees to turn up because there are typically people who can't make it at the last minute. But when more people arrive than I'd anticipated, the bar staff are happy to help me as I've already built a strong relationship with them.

Build a "Coffee Money" Fund

In Singapore, the term "coffee money" traditionally has negative connotations — it can mean a small bribe. In this context, however, I'm referring to the very different practice of regularly setting aside a little money to help fund your next networking event. Use it to buy that first round of drinks and food for your guests. People will remember your generosity, although it doesn't matter whether they reciprocate or not in the future.

I believe that hosting networking events can be beneficial for your career because it allows you to generate more social capital. In the future, people will be more willing to work with you when you need their help.

Part Four

Harness the Power of PIN: Persuasion, Impactful Communication, Negotiation

19

From "No" to "Yes" Using the 3Ps Method

Nobody likes the feeling of rejection. Over the years, I've developed a three-step process that converts situations from hopeless to hopeful. I call it the 3Ps approach:

Perseverance
Perspective
Positivity

Let me give you some examples of putting the 3Ps into action.

Leaving by 7 pm

Getting a table at some of Hong Kong's popular restaurants on a weekend can be as rare as winning the lottery. This is only a mild exaggeration. Like the folks who patiently queue up at lottery counters hoping to buy the winning ticket, I can't help but try my luck at my favorite Italian restaurant chain because its thin-crust pizzas and *aglio e olio* pasta are irresistible. My family often loves to dine at the busy Kennedy Town branch for dinner on Sunday. We usually make a spur-of-the-moment decision to go, and it's impossible to reserve a table on the same day. Well, almost impossible. I called the restaurant one Sunday afternoon, and a staff member picked up the phone promptly.

"Good afternoon!" a woman with a cheerful voice answered.

"Do you have a table for four tonight?" I asked hopefully.

"No sir, we're fully booked," she replied with a tinge of regret.

"How about at 6 pm?" I countered.

"Sir, we're fully booked," she repeated, probably thinking to herself, "which part of 'fully booked' do you not understand, sir?"

Undeterred, I proposed: "What if we leave by 7 pm?"

There was a slight pause on the other end of the line, as if she was unsure how to respond. "Let me check," she finally said. A few seconds later, she replied: "Yes sir, we have a table."

I'd used the 3Ps to change her mind, here's how:

Perseverance: Show Your Effort

I didn't hang up after she said, "fully booked". Instead, I came up with a counter proposal. When I suggested reaching the restaurant early I showed her I was willing to be flexible on timing.

Perspective: Understand the Other Person's Priority

The restaurant employee's main concern wasn't catering to my personal agenda; it was ensuring that customers who'd made reservations got their seats by the allotted time. She didn't care whether I wanted a table to celebrate my kid's birthday or my boss's resignation. Getting angry, saying how much business I've given the restaurant in the past, or threatening not to go there again weren't tactics that would appeal to her. Instead, I helped her do her job, by giving her the option to chase me out at 7 pm. An option, in the finance world, is a contract that gives the option holder the right (but not the obligation) to buy or sell a security at an agreed price. The restaurant employee here is the option holder. She had the right to ask me to leave at 7 pm, but on the night I wasn't actually shooed away because the restaurant had enough room, so the option holder didn't exercise her option.

Positivity

Call me an eternal optimist, but I'm always hopeful of flipping a situation from unfavorable to favorable. Most people would have been dejected when told that the restaurant was fully booked. Not me. I sought a compromise. Arriving at 6 pm and leaving at 7 pm was a win-win solution for both sides because the restaurant is rarely full during the early evening. I was helping it to utilize its resources more efficiently.

10 More Minutes

It's midnight. You're enjoying yourself hanging out and the night is still young for you — but not for your friend, Andrew. He wants to leave. How can you persuade him to stay until 1 am? If you simply ask him to hang around for another hour, he'll probably come up with excuses. But if you ask him to stay for just 10 more minutes and offer to buy him a drink, he's more likely to oblige. During this 10 minutes, introduce some interesting apps or people to him, so he won't even realize that time has flown by. By 12.30 am, offer to shout him a taxi home, and then leave at 12.45 am. "Didn't you say till 1 am?" I did, but you also need to compromise.

The 3Ps are applicable in this example.

Perseverance: Show Your Effort

When you asked Andrew to stay for 10 minutes and offered to buy him a drink, you were showing him that you valued his company.

Perspective: Understand the Person's Priority

Andrew was expecting to have a good time when he agreed to hang out with you and your friends. When he decided to leave early, he was most likely not having fun, and didn't want to waste another hour with you. But 10 more minutes didn't sound very painful, so he agreed. You gave him the *option* to leave in 10 minutes.

Positivity

Because you were hopeful, your cheerfulness showed and was infectious, signaling to Andrew that the next 10 minutes would be more enjoyable for him. Some may ask, "won't friends feel cheated that they stayed longer than they thought they would?" I disagree! They aren't trapped. They can leave after 10 minutes but choose not to, so they're obviously having a good time.

Can I Drop by?

The ability to change a "no" to a "yes" is even more crucial in the workplace. When I was working for a bank, a corporate client based in Taipei asked for a renminbi (RMB) construction loan to build an office tower in Shanghai. This was a 10-year loan and my colleague from the loans department priced it accordingly, using the five-year or longer rate of 5.94% (see table below that shows the People's Bank of China's, PBOC, loan rates in 2009).

2009	THE PEOPLE'S BANK OF CHINA		
Financial Institutions:	Nominal Interest Rates		
Period	Time Deposits	Period	Loans
7 Days	1.35		
3 Months	1.71	6 Months or Less	4.86
6 Months	1.98	1 Year or Less	5.31
1 Year	2.25	3 Years or Less	5.40
3 Years	3.33	5 Years or Less	5.76
5 Years	3.60	5 Years or Longer	5.94

In the cutthroat world of finance, another bank offered this client what I call a "creative" loan structure. Instead of the standard 10-year loan, the bank proposed a six-month arrangement that would be continually extended until the loan was paid off at the end of 10 years. This shorter loan period had a much lower interest rate of 4.86%.

My colleague came to me to ask for solutions to resurrect the deal. I suggested a loan in U.S. dollars (USD) as well as a USD-RMB currency hedge to create a synthetic RMB loan with an all-in interest rate of 4.5%. It was cheaper than the other bank's offering but was still a 10-year loan. We quickly proposed our brilliant solution to the client's finance team. They liked it and submitted the idea to their CFO. The feedback was positive. I had saved the deal!

Our joy was short-lived. A week later, the client told us that they couldn't accept our proposal because their CFO had already verbally mandated the other bank even before hearing our innovative suggestion.

We were devastated. I couldn't understand why the client had chosen our competitor's more expensive solution, so I asked if I could "drop by" for a coffee meeting in Taipei. At the meeting, I explained that under mainland regulations, banks in China aren't allowed to price a long-term construction loan using the six-month PBOC lending rate. If the "creative" bank gets into trouble with the regulator, this may implicate its clients. The finance manager from the client firm noted what I'd said. I left the meeting and flew back to Hong Kong the same afternoon. The next day, the client called to say we'd got the deal. Again, the 3Ps are applicable here:

Perseverance: Show Your Effort

I continued to engage with the client even after they turned down our solution.

Perspective: Understand the Person's Priority

There were two possible "no's" here. First, the client could have said "no" to the face-to-face coffee meeting in Taipei. Had I stressed that I was making the business trip just to see them, they might not have agreed to the meeting because they might have felt obligated to reverse their decision if they met me. But when I asked "can I drop by?" they didn't feel as pressured. I gave them the option to say, "We won't change our loan mandate decision". This brings me to the second potential "no". I found out during the meeting that the CFO would lose face, if he withdrew his mandate from the other bank without a justification. By highlighting the non-compliant nature of that bank's proposal, I gave him a way out of his tight spot. Entering into a non-compliant financing structure doesn't sound like a risk worth taking.

Positivity

Despite having the door slammed shut when our competitor won the loan mandate, I still made the trip to Taipei and remained hopeful I could do a deal.

We're likely to receive more rejections than approvals during our lives. People will say "no" to us more than they say "yes". But to achieve big things, we should use the 3Ps method to persuade others and reject rejection.

20

Making Bourbon and Cokes

I wasn't aware of the importance of internships when I was a university student, so I didn't spend my holidays toiling away in an office. During one of my school breaks, I took an assistant bartender job at Fire Disco, which back then was a popular nightclub on Singapore's famous Orchard Road. My basic salary was only $650 a month, but I was happy to be earning money and I've proudly kept my Fire employment contract until this day. Housing easily a thousand people, the mega club had two levels and I usually worked on the upper floor's island bar, which was oval-shaped and surrounded by a sea of partygoers.

On my first day of work, I was given a copy of a handwritten list of cocktail recipes and asked to memorize them. In three days, as if preparing for university entrance exams, I learned how to make all the cocktails, and memorized the type of glass (highball, champagne saucer, rocks glass etc.) and the number of coupons each drink required. While standard fare like wine and beer were worth one coupon, most cocktails cost between two and four. You'd need to hand over six coupons for our most potent beverage, which was ominously called "graveyard" and would knock out even the best drinker.

While the resident rock band belted out songs from the likes of Guns N' Roses and the Eagles, I prepared garnishes for drinks and got the bar ready. As soon as the band stopped for a short break, customers rushed toward the bar waving multiple blue drinks coupons and ordering cocktails like screwdrivers, Long Island iced teas and Singapore slings.

Trying to outdo the loud music, one customer shouted "Kahlua milk" across the counter. I quickly ran through in my head the list of cocktails that I'd memorized the previous nights, but I couldn't recall this one. Too embarrassed to ask the customer for clarification, I turned around and asked a fellow bartender at the station behind me. He replied, "Brown cow!" I knew the brown cow cocktail: one jigger of Kahlua topped up with milk. It had been on my list after all, but because the customer had called it by a different name, I'd been at a complete loss. Being exam smart hadn't helped me.

Despite my diligence, my inexperience as a bartender continued to hold me back during my first few days on the job. I couldn't cope with the sudden surges in demand whenever the band stopped playing. No matter how quickly I made the drinks, it was never fast enough to clear the crowd. When the band came back on stage, many customers left the bar disappointed and thirsty. After a week or so of ineptitude, I was working on a Saturday evening and facing many customers clamoring for my attention. One of them called out, "rainbow", a complicated cocktail made up of seven separate layers of liquor and syrup. It would easily take five minutes for me to make this colorful drink without mistakenly blending the ingredients together.

I suddenly paused from fixing my drinks, stood up straight, looked directly at the crowd and said, "I'm going to make bourbon Coke now. Who wants one!?" Half of the customers, including the person who'd asked for the rainbow, changed their orders to bourbon and Coke. I counted 12 orders, laid out a row of glasses, added ice, and poured bourbon continuously from the first to the final glass, and then picked up the soda gun to inject the Coke. The partying people gladly exchanged their coupons for drinks they didn't know they'd be ordering until a minute earlier. I then went on to make gin and tonics, the next most popular drink at the club.

The customers were happy because they got their drinks fast, and so was my manager because that meant more drinks were sold. I was happy that I could satisfy both my customers and my boss. This experience taught me that sometimes people don't know what they really want or what they're prepared to accept. The Fire Disco patrons essentially wanted a nice drink that could be served within two minutes, but there wasn't such an item on the menu… until I created it by standardizing my orders.

This lesson doesn't just apply to bartenders. I worked in sales and trading for several years earlier in my banking career. Transactions took place in a matter of seconds or minutes. The dealing room environment, especially back then, was fast-paced, exciting and noisy. Traders would shout currency prices, salespeople would speak to clients over the phone, and the Reuters screen would flash up the latest market-moving news.

I structured interest rate and currency options to help corporate clients manage their financial risk. Like cocktails, these options were usually tailor-made to suit the needs of individual clients. But when a certain currency became "hot", demand to hedge risk might suddenly surge and we wouldn't have enough staff to cope with the number of enquiries we were receiving. Clients would then complain about our slow response times. Knowing some clients were under time pressure from their bosses, we went on to standardize some features of our products. We convinced clients to accept these non-bespoke products, so we could price them faster. Clients were able to execute their hedging solutions before FX prices moved against them, which kept their bosses happy. I couldn't help thinking back to my Fire Disco days: you can influence people's decisions if you understand their most urgent needs.

21

Is the Delivery Cost Worth It?

Cintha was carrying a big can of popcorn and had an equally big smile on her face as she joined me and our other friends for a get-together. She unwrapped the popcorn, which had been flown all the way from Chicago, and then shared her favorite treat with us. This was more than 20 years ago, when large boxes of popcorn were a rare sight in Singapore. I'd certainly never come across one so huge.

Even though I don't have a sweet tooth, the popcorn tasted really nice. But I was more interested in where it had come from than the popcorn itself. We "interrogated" Cintha about who had given her the treat that had made her so happy. Cintha, who is from Indonesia but had been studying in America, confessed that the present was from a boy in the U.S. who knew all about her love of popcorn.

At that time, Amazon hadn't ventured beyond selling books, so the cost of delivering the gift from Chicago to Singapore must have been a lot more than the price of the popcorn. My immediate reaction was incomprehension: no matter how delicious the popcorn was, I couldn't work out why someone would spend so much sending it halfway around the world. Perhaps because of my engineering education — I was taught to think in terms of numbers — I didn't place enough value on human emotions. I eventually understood that the delivery fee was definitely worth it because the present had made Cintha so happy. In a wider sense, this incident has also made me realize the big impact of doing small things well, if you want to impress someone special in your life, or demonstrate your competence at work.

Today, I often want my coaching clients to experience the importance of doing small things well. One of these clients is Ming, a motivated young professional who works in risk management. During our first session, he told me he wanted to make more connections with senior people in the finance sector. By the end of our Zoom call, I promised to send him a copy of the latest editions of the *Economist* and *Financial Times*. Just 40 minutes later, a delivery man was standing outside his front door with copies of the two publications. It had cost me about $20, more than the combined value of the magazine and newspaper, to send a courier bike to Ming's house. But he was impressed that I'd made the effort of arranging the quick delivery. I hope this experience showed Ming that if he does small things well, he too can make a big impression on others, including senior people.

During the middle of my banking career, I was seconded to Shanghai and tasked with setting up a derivative structuring desk. Before one of my business trips I asked Yan, one of the few interns under my charge, to photocopy the business cards of three clients whom I planned to visit in another part of the country. In China, business cards usually have English on one side and Chinese on the other. Most people would have taken the easier option and copied the English side of those business cards onto one piece of paper and the Chinese side onto another. But Yan put both versions on just one sheet by photocopying the Chinese text first and then re-photocopying it alongside the English text. I later decided to offer Yan a full-time job at the bank, partly because her small and considerate action showed me she would take good care of clients.

In many sectors, juniors can quickly learn the technical aspects of the role, so it's often the extra little steps you take beyond your job responsibilities that help you get ahead. You should use your initiative, like Yan did. If you hear that your boss needs to book a restaurant near the office of an important client, offer to research suitable restaurants and make the booking. Junior professionals sometimes think that tasks like restaurant bookings are too menial for them to bother with. But if you can't do minor tasks well, you won't get a chance to do the more important work because people won't trust you to do a good job. Conversely, when you put effort into small things, it sends a message to your bosses and colleagues that you can do big things even better.

22

Most Valuable Player vs Most Improved Player

The art of communicating well isn't always about how you influence those around you. Sometimes you need to change the way you communicate with yourself before you can deal effectively with others.

Back in 2011, I left a large universal bank to become a managing director at the Hong Kong office of a top-tier investment bank (also known as a "bulge bracket" firm in the world of investment banking). I experienced a step-up in my job rank, and more importantly, a big change in my working environment. I soon began to develop feelings of inadequacy, even though I had the technical skills for the job. Quite a few people in my department had an elite upbringing: they came from wealthy families or had attended top Western or Chinese universities, or both. But I had graduated from a local college in Singapore and was the son of a street food vendor.

One of my juniors was a Yale and Peking University alumna who spoke three languages fluently and was extremely polished and professional in everything she did. Among the privileged group, a couple were super rich and had grown up within the very upper echelons of society.

I hadn't encountered many of these people before in my banking career. When I was working in a dealing room, for example, many of my colleagues were local grads because you don't typically need a foreign education to do this kind of job. In corporate sales, I was mainly selling to local businesses. Investment banking was a whole new ball game. Now I was meeting business owners and CEOs of much larger corporations. Perhaps it was no wonder that I sometimes felt a bit out of my depth.

During my first year at the bulge bracket, Chuck, a friend of mine from another bank, began introducing me to a few people within his network in Hong Kong. "You have to listen to Eric's story!" he'd say, before briefly telling them how I'd risen from humble beginnings to become a managing director at a top investment bank. To him, that was a great story. After Chuck had done this numerous times, I began to think: was my story actually interesting rather than inadequate? When I eventually decided that Chuck was correct, I became comfortable with my background, despite the elite world I was now working in. Chuck had inadvertently helped me change the way I saw myself.

Some of my previous feelings of inadequacy had come about because I'd put myself in an unnecessarily difficult position. To use a sporting analogy, I'd tried to be the most valuable player (MVP) in my division. However, my family and educational background made this a nearly impossible goal because I couldn't compete with my more elite colleagues, who had a much wider and deeper network of potential clients. I decided instead to change my objective: I now wanted to become the most improved player (MIP) — the banker who was increasingly making a name for himself. This was a target that I could, and did, achieve.

As soon as I changed my thinking, I also realized that most elite people (both colleagues and clients) are either interested in how people like me have climbed up the career ladder, or they simply don't care about our backgrounds as long as we perform well on the job. The fact that I was even hired to work alongside them proves this point. Since I took the small action of refocusing how I view myself, I've become more comfortable with sharing my failures, and more willing to tell people about some of the highs and lows of my childhood and early adulthood. As a result, I have more stories to share in my new career as a coach, lecturer and writer. Being able to communicate in a more authentic manner with myself means I'm now able to converse better with a wider range of people.

I hope this story will help you to be comfortable with your own background because it shows how you can move forward in your career, no matter where you came from. Remember that many people you meet don't even care about your social status because they have too many other things to worry about. If you start to feel inadequate like I once did, it's probably your own thinking that you might want to change. Ultimately, the most important story is the one you tell yourself.

23
Never Wear a Chicken Suit

I was pretty clueless in my mid-20s when it came to formal dressing. After I completed my master's degree at Lancaster University in the U.K., I set my heart on getting a banking job in the City of London. I was fortunate enough to land interviews at several banks and I spent a lot of time preparing for them. But there was one problem: I didn't own a suit. Up until that point in time, I hadn't needed to wear one. In Singapore, a long-sleeve shirt and tie were good enough for job interviews and work.

I didn't have much money to spend on clothes, so I went to Oxfam, a cut-price charity shop, to look for a second-hand jacket. The store didn't have my size, so I ended up buying a jacket so big that I could have hidden a chicken inside it. I arrived at the interviews in my "chicken" suit jacket and a pair of non-matching pants. By contrast, my interviewers were impeccably dressed, as were the other candidates. Truth be told, all the interviews ended quickly, and I didn't hear back from any of the companies. Perhaps there were other reasons for my failure — my degree and work experience might not have been good enough to land a role in London — but my clothes certainly didn't help create a good first impression.

While I had done some thorough research on the technical aspects of the jobs on offer, I didn't fully understand the culture of the country or of the banks. In the U.K., bankers dress formally. As soon as I walked into the interviews, the British bankers could tell that I didn't fit in. While I couldn't have afforded a high-end tailored suit, investing some of my last-remaining savings into a decent off-the-rack one would have ensured that they judged me more on my merits than my appearance.

I learned from the mistake I made in London, and I'm now trying to teach my coaching clients about the importance of making positive first impressions at work. One of my clients, Edwin, has 10 years' experience at big technology firms, and he recently fulfilled his ambition to join a large financial institution in a middle management tech role. When I was preparing him for his new job in the financial sector, he said he was planning to turn up at work on his first day in a black T-shirt and casual pants, the outfit he'd worn all the time at the tech companies. I suggested that this would create a poor first impression and advised him to instead wear a smart jacket and pants. While this outfit is less formal than a suit, it would still help him fit into the banking culture.

After his first day on the job, Edwin called to thank me. He was surprised that I'd got the dress code at his firm spot on. Edwin said people he randomly passed in the office even acknowledged him (by nodding or saying hello), which had never happened to him before when starting a new role. The way he presented himself had immediately created the right impression.

If he'd dressed too casually, his new banking colleagues might have mistaken him for a delivery man rather than someone who was capable of leading a team. As a manager, this would have been a terrible first impression to make. While Edwin had been hired because of the innovative experience he'd gained at two big tech firms, it would have been unwise for him to appear like he was still working for one. His job involves liaising with front-office people, who all dress conservatively, so Edwin had to adapt his clothes accordingly.

Making a good first impression with your appearance doesn't mean you have to rush out and buy a super expensive suit or blouse, but it does mean dressing appropriately for the role you're in, especially if it's a new job. Some young people I talk to are under the false impression that how we dress is no longer important and that all businesses are embracing an anything-goes culture. But Edwin's example shows that this isn't the case: how you look is a vital aspect of how you communicate to others.

Dressing nicely also shows respect to the people you're meeting. If you ask people whether they judge you by your appearance, the answer is almost always "no", but subconsciously what they think of you is affected by how you dress, especially the first couple of times they see you. Never wear a chicken suit or ill-fitting clothes!

24

How to Deliver a TEDx Talk

Fear of public speaking is so common that there's a word for it: glossophobia. But if you can overcome your anxieties about speaking to an audience, you can advance your career and make yourself better known in your industry. If you eventually become a really confident speaker, you can influence others with what you say.

I didn't always enjoy speaking in public. As a young person and up until my early 30s, I suffered from stage fright when asked to make a presentation. That wasn't great for my career. When I was a vice president (VP) at an American bank, my boss went on holiday and asked me to present the weekly market update to the sales and structuring teams across Asia on his behalf. I told him I couldn't host the meeting because I was busy preparing for my Professional Risk Manager (PRM) exams. But this was just an excuse. In reality, I was simply too scared to make the presentation. He got another VP to do it instead. By year end, when it came to promotion nominations, guess who my manager chose to promote to director level? That's right, not me, but the other VP.

If you perform well in your job, but don't speak up in meetings, you're making it difficult for managers to know about your work. Even if your own boss wants to promote you, no one else in the company will support you because they hardly know you. It comes down to this simple equation:

How good you are × your presentation skills = how good people think you are.

Public speaking, whether in a small team meeting or a giant lecture hall, gives you more exposure to senior people. When you make a compelling presentation, people can picture you as a senior manager who has the ability to lead a team.

I took small steps to overcome my fear of public speaking. The first target I set myself was to speak for just 10 minutes in front of about 10 colleagues. This gave me the confidence to run larger training sessions at my bank. I then ventured out of the office to teach at universities, and eventually I gave my first TEDx talk, which was a pretty scary experience. Knowing that the camera was rolling as I delivered my speech on the famous round red carpet made me nervous. I'd rehearsed no less than 50 times, but I did so badly that I wished the talk hadn't been recorded.

When I was invited to give my second TEDx a year later, I wasn't sure if I could take another poor performance. The organizer, Tommy, suggested that I tell my personal story. "Are you sure?" I asked. He said the fact that I was invited to speak at a TEDx event meant my story was worth sharing. I delivered my speech, "10 years of selling noodles", to a packed university auditorium in Hong Kong. The feedback was positive, and I felt much better about my performance. I realized the key to successful public speaking is having a story worth sharing. Practice is also important; there are no shortcuts. Below are some tips to help you deliver a TEDx talk, or any presentation to an audience.

Visualize

During my banking days, I often went to big conferences in swanky hotels. When the session was over for the day and participants had left the ballroom, I'd walk onto the stage. I'd pretend to be looking for something there in case a member of the production crew asked me what I was doing. When no one was looking, I'd face the almost empty ballroom and visualize myself as a presenter speaking to a hall packed with people. I'd try to get used to the lighting as well. When you get a chance, you can do the same.

Use Props

Props can easily catch the attention of your audience and make you stand out from other speakers because most people don't bother using them.

I remember watching my university finance lecturer putting a tiny cocktail umbrella over his balding head to illustrate how U.S. and European banks carried too little capital to weather their catastrophic losses during the Asian financial crisis in 1997. I can still clearly remember him and his lecture because of his prop.

Build Rapport with Your Audience

The CFA Society Bahrain invited me to give a talk on "developing thinking and skills in the world of disruptive innovation". I'd never been to Bahrain, so I flew in a day before my talk to get to know a bit about the country and its culture and people. As you'll remember from Chapter 14, after checking in at the conference hotel, I took a taxi and asked the driver to take me to any well-known place for local food, adding that I like rice and chicken dishes. He dropped me off at Mohammed Noor, a casual eatery not far from my hotel, and I ordered a charcoal-grilled chicken biryani. It was out of this world: the best biryani I've had in my life. When I shared my dining experience with the CFA audience at the start of my keynote speech the next day, I got some good laughter and applause. The crowd was amazing! Many people came forward after my presentation to give me terrifically positive feedback. I attributed the success of my talk largely to my curiosity about the Bahraini culture and to trusting the taste of the local taxi driver.

Facts Tell, Stories Sell

Audiences remember interesting stories better than bare facts, so I usually use stories to illustrate my points. When I teach banking and finance courses at universities, I talk about the deals I've done. Without mentioning clients' names, I tell students how I managed to land deals or why I sometimes lost out to competitors. You can learn more about storytelling techniques in Chapter 37.

Make It an Entertaining Show

You might have noticed that I often refer to the people attending my presentations as the "audience" (instead of participants, delegates etc.). That's because as presenters we're supposed to *entertain* as well as educate.

Sometimes audiences travel from afar to hear us speak, so they deserve to have a good time. I prepare my talks as if they're a show for my audience. I once did a short presentation on healthy cooking for busy professionals. Instead of just lecturing, I prepared a salad from scratch in front of everyone.

Be Audience Specific

I once made a presentation to an expat women's group on time management, and I told them that I only wear white shirts to the office to save the trouble of choosing a color every morning. They weren't pleased, to say the least. If they'd had eggs in their hands, they would have thrown them at me. "Women can't wear the same color to work every day!" many of them remarked. Lesson learned. Since that day, I've always made my talks specific to the audience. When I lecture at Peking University, I speak in Mandarin and use examples from China and Chinese culture. When I gave a presentation at Cambridge University, I started by talking about Mr Lee Kuan Yew, Singapore's first Prime Minister, because he graduated from Cambridge in 1949. I showed the students a photo of him and his wife standing in front of the university's famous Bridge of Sighs.

Record Your Presentation

When you want to make rapid improvements to your presentation style, you can set up a video camera to record your speech to evaluate later. It's weird to hear your own voice on video, but if you can get over any embarrassment, reviewing your own video recording is an effective way to improve your public speaking without hiring a speaking coach.

If you're just starting out making presentations, there's no need to use all these tips immediately. I'd suggest picking one or two of them each time you do a speech. Soon you'll develop your own public speaking style and will be engaging well with your audience. One day you might also get to deliver your own TEDx talk. Remember: while your presentation style is important, your success as a speaker ultimately depends on having a great story to share.

25
You Need ESP

We're all expected to present over video these days, so we all need ESP. No, I don't mean extra sensory perception; I'm referring to the expertise, showmanship, and production skills required to come across well on video platforms.

Having expertise in your field will allow you to speak with authority, but that won't be enough to impress your online audience. You must also present yourself and your ideas clearly and with flair (showmanship) and your video production must be of high quality. It's the third part of ESP (production) that many of us overlook. Even if you're a polished speaker on stage, you won't necessarily do well in front of a virtual audience, especially if your audio quality and lighting are poor.

Some candidates fail job interviews via video, but would have aced them in person. They prepare great answers, but pay little attention to the technical production aspects. As online interviews become more common, having a decent laptop and stable internet connection aren't enough to set you apart. I'd recommend you go further and invest in some extra equipment (see the tips below for details) to ensure you make a good impression.

This advice also applies when you present to clients, colleagues or webinar attendees. If you perform strongly during these presentations,

you'll improve your reputation as a tech-savvy person. Getting the basics of production right isn't difficult (there are a few small actions to take), but not many people make the effort, so you'll stand out if you do. The pandemic forced me to step up my own game as I began to host more webinars and speak at online conferences. I've incorporated new technology and techniques into my video presentations, so I know that having good equipment (and using it well) can make a big impact. Here are seven basic tips you should try out.

How to Make a Good Impression on Video Calls

Make Sure Your Camera is at Eye Level

If your laptop is just sitting on your desk, its camera will be much lower than your eyes, and the other people on the call will be looking up your nostrils! You can trim your nostril hair… or raise the height of the camera to eye level by placing your computer on a laptop stand. Basic stands are inexpensive, but a couple of thick books underneath your laptop will also do the job.

Get a Digital Camera With a Changeable Lens

Raising the height of your laptop's in-built camera will improve how you look on screen, but if you really want to impress interviewers, colleagues and clients, you'll need an external camera. Consider a changeable lens digital camera because it will allow you to adjust the width of the view to show only what you want people to see, keeping the untidy part of your room out of sight. This kind of camera will focus on you while keeping the background soft to give you a professional look. It's worth the investment, if you can afford it.

Never Use Your Laptop Mic

Great audio is even more important than great video. Never use your computer's microphone! It picks up background noise and you also get reverberance (echo). If you're a candidate and interviewers struggle to hear you, it will be difficult for them to assess you, no matter how qualified you are. I use a condenser USB mic, but you could also consider buying good quality noise cancelling headphones.

Get the Lighting Right

We've all seen people use a sunny window or a white wall as their background on video calls. But this can mean their face isn't lit up enough because cameras set their brightness based on the average brightness of the whole image. You should position yourself next to (rather than in front of) a window, so that one side of your face is slightly brighter than the other. This is known as the Rembrandt lighting setup, and it gives your face some depth. If there's no window, use a desk lamp to bounce light off a wall and light up one side of your face. Even a small and cheap video light can dramatically improve the quality of your video.

Showcase Your Backdrop

Forget about using a virtual background; use a real backdrop in your home to your advantage by showcasing your personality and interests. For example, you could display books, plants, and that trophy you just won. An appropriate, uncluttered and creative arrangement will help you stand out.

Smile and Raise Your Hands

Other people on the call can't see your full body to read your body language or gauge your enthusiasm, so smile more than usual to demonstrate that you're interested in what they're saying. Show your hands on the screen a few times during the call to win trust. You'll need to raise your hands to ear level for them to be visible.

Share Your Work

If you're doing an online interview, be prepared to share some (non-confidential) sample work with your interviewers, so that you can say, "I did some simulation models during my master's program — may I show you my spreadsheet?" During a work meeting or client call, sharing your laptop's screen is commonplace. But you can still impress your audience by sharing your phone or tablet's screen via a mirroring app like Reflector. I've also started pulling up images next to my face during presentations to make tech my differentiator.

Why and How to Make a Video CV/Biography

The video CV, a short film about your achievements and ambitions, is becoming a more important part of your arsenal as a job seeker. An increasing number of employers are requesting one, but even those that don't will be impressed if you include one in your application. A video CV (referred to in some countries as a video resume) can also be used for marketing — e.g. as a biography to send to new clients, or as a profile if you're speaking at a conference. Here are seven key steps you should follow to produce a video CV.

Step 1. Create Content

Choose three to five points from your written CV to talk about, but give them a new twist by including two or three additional benefits that you bring to an employer — for example, you can attract new customers or provide new product knowledge. If I wanted to show the advantages of hiring me as a speaker, I'd say, "I'll help you attract attendees to your event, and I'll keep your audience engaged not just with interesting content, but also with high quality production". It's a good idea to add a story about yourself to make your video CV more memorable.

Step 2. Write Your Script

Script out what you plan to say, and add it to a teleprompter (you can download a free teleprompter app to your mobile phone or tablet). Read it out loud and edit your script until it sounds natural.

Step 3. Record Audio Only

Continue practicing by recording just your audio. Play it back and listen to how you sound. If you rarely listen to your own recorded voice, you may have to hear the audio a few times to accept the way you sound. I initially refused to listen to the recording of my first TEDx talk!

Step 4. Prepare Slides and Photos

Prepare some slides and photos to add to your video. For example, slides showing logos of your schools and previous employers, and photos of you engaging in work or leisure activities.

Step 5. Shoot

Use your phone or camera to shoot a video of yourself using the script you've prepared.

Step 6. Edit

Edit your video. Add the slides and photos.

Step 7. Save and Share

Save your video on a sharable platform like Google Drive. Add the link to your written CV/resume.

Making a video CV is a great skill in itself. When you hear and see yourself on video, especially after multiple takes of fine-tuning your speech, you'll become a much better presenter. I think the ability to make a good recorded presentation will very soon become as important as the ability to speak confidently in front of a live audience. If you can make a great video CV today, your skill set will stay ahead of the curve.

Part Five

Remember:
You're Really a Salesperson

26

The Seven Steps of Selling Yourself

In our careers, we're essentially selling ourselves — our services and time — to the companies we work for or want to join. But too often we don't go about self-promotion effectively enough to land those sought-after new jobs or rise up the ranks at our current firms. As an engineer by training, I didn't initially like selling when I entered the workforce. Cliches about snake oil and used cars came to my mind. But I ended up selling financial products and services for more than 20 years, and I realized that I could adapt these selling skills to help my students get ahead in their careers.

Having a selling mindset can help you achieve your career goals, so I've come up with seven steps for successfully selling yourself. While I've explained them by focusing on the process of finding a new job, they can be used at other stages of your career, such as when you're seeking an overseas transfer or planning a new business venture.

The selling guide below is referenced in other chapters in this section of the book. Please refer back to it when you need to.

Follow Up | Identify Targets
07 | 01
Execute 06 | **Seven Steps of Selling Yourself** | 02 | Build Rapport & Trust
Overcome Objections 05 | 03 | Identify Needs & Problems
04
Present Solutions

Step 1: Identify Your Targets

When you're first thinking about getting a new job, you should target two groups of people: insiders and connectors. Insiders are employees of the companies you want to join and people who are already doing the type of roles you aspire to work in. They're in the know, and can give you information about the culture of their organizations, the requirements of relevant jobs, and the setup and reporting lines of their department. Connectors are people who can connect you to jobs. You'd be surprised at how often companies find candidates within their employees' wider networks. When I want to hire, besides advertising on job portals, I ask for candidate referrals from teammates, people in other departments, ex-colleagues, business partners and clients. I also approach university career advisors because they may know students and alumni with the experience that I'm looking for. Both insiders and connectors (these groups can sometimes overlap) are likely to be on LinkedIn.

Step 2: Build Rapport and Trust With the Target Group

You've identified your targets, now comes a more challenging step in your sales journey: building rapport with them. Read their posts and engage with them on LinkedIn, and try to get to know them in person too, for example by buying them coffee to discuss industry trends, or inviting them to speak at your university, organization or interest group. Offer to help them, if you can. Establishing rapport with just a couple of contacts will provide you with valuable information, so don't get disheartened if most people turn you down. The process of building rapport and trust could take a year or two. Don't expect to start now and land a great job next month. For more advice on how to build rapport and trust, please see Part 3, which is devoted to social capital.

Step 3: Identify Their Underlying Needs

If you want to work in a particular company, you need to do some advanced due diligence to understand its needs. Ask insiders about the typical profile of the people they hire. Perhaps their firm wants candidates with expertise in Asian languages, or perhaps presentation skills are critical because the hiring process involves a case-study presentation. Sometimes the requirements will be quite specific. Your insider might tell you that their company is planning to recruit people who can utilize data-driven approaches to conduct market research. Try to find out about the company culture, too. Is there a dog-eat-dog ethos in the office? Is hiring and firing a common practice? Knowing the culture of the organization will help you decide whether to apply for a job there. It will also help you prepare for interviews, and ensure you know what to expect if you decide to join.

Step 4: Present Solutions

Your connectors tell you about a job at the company and you land an interview. Congratulations! The interview is the time to make use of the due diligence you've done over the past year. You already know the employer's needs, so you now present a solution: you. If you've been told that the firm's culture emphasizes creativity, don't just say at the interview that you're creative; use a story (see Chapter 37) to explain how you've taken a creative approach to solving a problem. Remember to sell your benefits as a candidate (Chapter 27), and to showcase your skills, for example by taking your iPad to the interview with a sample of your work (without breaching confidentiality).

Step 5: Anticipate and Overcome Objections

You're unlikely to be the perfect candidate who meets all the criteria of the job. If you are, you should be concerned because there will be no room for you to grow in the role. You should prepare in advance to deal with an interviewer's objections. If you're honest about your weaknesses (Chapter 35), you can pre-empt their doubts about you and have a well-honed rebuttal. If your fluency in Mandarin Chinese needs improving, for example, highlight the fact that you've been studying business-level Mandarin, watching a lot of Chinese movies, and regularly using Chinese social media.

Step 6: Execute

If you get an informal verbal job offer, now is not the time to relax or assume that the role is in the bag. I've seen plenty of seemingly secure jobs fall through before the new recruit signs their employment contract. The company could suddenly freeze its headcount, fail to secure a work visa, or find another candidate at the last minute. This is why you need to stay in touch with the hiring manager in the run-up to receiving a written offer. If they see that you're a persistent and committed candidate, they'll be more likely to ask their head office for an exemption from the freeze, lodge an appeal to secure you a visa, or rate you ahead of the new applicant. You should also get ready to submit names of two referees because the hiring company is likely to ask for them.

Step 7: Follow Up

You've now signed a written job offer. You're waiting to finish your degree course or seeing out your notice period at your current firm. Don't rest on your laurels or take a long holiday. The weeks or months before you start a job are the perfect time to ensure you can deliver on what you sold the new company during the interview. For example, if you told the interviewer you'd improve your programming skills, follow up on this and take a training course.

The above steps to selling yourself aren't a one-off exercise. After you've been in your new position for six months, start planning for a promotion or job transfer to another department three years down the road. Identify people who could help you achieve that, and tweak the selling process with an internal move in mind. Keep on repeating the cycle if you want to continue advancing your career.

27

Sell Benefits, Not Features During Job Interviews

Before we dive deep into step four (present solutions) from Chapter 26, let's imagine you work in retail sales and have been asked to sell luxury Italian-made loafers (slip-on style shoes) designed specifically for driving. The shoes retail for around $500 a pair. How do you promote footwear that's so expensive?

One way might be to draw attention to the technical features, like the rubber-studded sole that helps prevent your feet from slipping when you hit the accelerator while driving a sports car whose seats are slung low to the floor. But at the end of the day, these features may not be exclusive enough to land you the sale, and the shoe's appearance isn't dissimilar to a standard slip-on design. If you want to convince people to part with their money and reach them on an emotional level, it's more effective to concentrate on selling them *benefits*.

People who purchase driving shoes usually love and spend a lot of money on their cars. So when you sell these loafers, you should tell potential customers that what they're considering buying is a unique extension of their vehicle. Even when they're not sitting in their exotic sports car, they can still feel like the car is with them by wearing the shoe — that's the big benefit for them. Some people like to put their car key on a restaurant table to show off what they're driving, but shoes are a more subtle way to open up a conversation about a cherished automobile. When you reframe the shoe as a must-have car accessory and highlight the benefits this brings to a car lover, $500 suddenly seems relatively cheap compared with the hundreds of thousands of dollars they've spent on the car itself.

We can also focus on benefits rather than features in our careers, especially when it comes to presenting solutions to our employer's problems (step four of my selling guide). Let me give you three examples.

A Hong Kong Transfer

After I'd been working in the sales and trading team of my bank in Shanghai for a while, my boss encouraged me to apply for a transfer into the global capital markets unit in Hong Kong. But it wasn't a straightforward move: I was competing against two other internal candidates, and I'd have to interview with a Hong Kong hiring manager who didn't know me.

How did I "sell" myself to the manager? The key features I could offer him were my financial product knowledge, engineering degree and quantitative skills, but I didn't think these would be enough to get me the job, so I decided to turn my quant expertise into a benefit. I explained that I'd developed quantitative tools to identify the risk exposure of corporate clients. The benefit of him hiring me was that I could use these exclusive tools to perform financial risk analysis on clients, and propose capital market solutions for them. I could help him sell not just my products, but other products under his charge. Competing candidates for the Hong Kong job were likely focusing on their strong product knowledge, but that's just a feature which other people in the company might also possess. When I sold my unique benefit — helping the firm and its clients via my analytical tools — the boss liked what he heard… and I got the job.

When Excel Becomes a Benefit

Having advanced Excel skills may be required in your job, but even if VBA programming or using the VLOOKUP function is your forte, that still counts as a feature. To convert it into a benefit, you should tell your boss (or an interviewer looking to hire you) that you're able to use Excel to automate some of the repetitive tasks that the team is doing. That will benefit the team members by freeing up their time for more productive work.

Get Flexible

When I speak to young professionals or read their LinkedIn profiles, a lot of them describe themselves as "hard working and conscientious". But these traits are features; they don't explain how their company benefits from an employee's industriousness. If you're young and don't have children yet, you could say that you're flexible and can work late whenever there are urgent tasks to be done. Your boss will clearly see the advantages in that.

The small action of turning a feature into a benefit will open up opportunities within your own company and help you when you're job hunting. But too often our CVs/resumes and LinkedIn profiles merely state our years of experience and list our features (our job duties, skills and qualifications) without mentioning how our contributions benefited our employers. Having 10 years' experience is meaningless unless you articulate the value of your work.

You can begin the process of turning your features into benefits straight away. Choose some features from your CV (for example, you're bilingual, know how to write computer programs, and enjoy customer service) then spend some time trying to work out the current or potential benefits of each one.

Sell benefits, not features.

28
Chocolate Instead

You've secured the job you want, and you're now eyeing your next promotion or pitching new proposals to colleagues. No matter how good you think you are at selling yourself and your ideas, you'll always come up against barriers and objections. One of the lessons I've learned from the setbacks I've suffered is that to overcome obstacles more easily (see step five in the selling guide from Chapter 26), you should build strong levels of rapport with colleagues and industry counterparts. The stronger the rapport (step two), the easier it is to overcome the objections.

Unfortunately, too many of us view rapport as a short-term concept, and try to create it only when there's an immediate, selfish gain to be had. But relationships don't work like that. You need to play a long game, and give more than you take. You don't have to give a lot: doing small things well is often enough to build rapport and trust, as you'll see in the following examples.

Know People's Life Status

Understanding the life status of the person you're building a rapport with is just as important as getting to know their cultural background and career history. Someone who's recently had a baby is unlikely to accept an invitation to evening drinks, but may agree to have lunch with you. When I work with young professionals, I often create networking events for them because I know that meeting new people is important at that stage of their lives.

Many years ago, I met up with my friend Sue and we chatted over lunch about her children and what they enjoyed doing. I told her about *Charlie and Lola*, a British cartoon about the antics of two siblings that were around the same ages as her son and daughter. Sue was keen for her kids to see the show, so after our meal I bought the first episode of *Charlie and Lola* on DVD, and couriered it to her office. Her kids loved it and her husband went out to purchase the rest of the series. Buying a small and thoughtful gift, which is tailored to someone's status in life, can help you build rapport.

Buy Timely Gifts

When buying gifts to build rapport, you should also make them well-timed. When I was working in banking, my team and I had a morning meeting with an important real-estate developer client to pitch a derivatives idea about hedging exposure for a commercial property loan. The developer's CFO, Henry, said we were too late to land the deal because other banks had bought him mooncakes, a sweet Chinese treat traditionally enjoyed during the Mid-Autumn Festival. "The mooncakes are already in my stomach," he said, in a seemingly joking manner.

When we returned to the office, I asked my colleague to buy some mooncakes for Henry, but she couldn't find any because the festival was over. I suggested a box of chocolates instead. When she said she'd buy it later in the week, I told her not to wait and to get the gift to Henry that same afternoon. Shortly after lunchtime we received a thank-you email from Henry saying he really appreciated our efforts in sending over the chocolates so quickly, and he was pulling our legs when he mentioned the mooncakes. Don't be fooled! Oftentimes, when people want to deliver an unpleasant message to you, they disguise it as a joke. Henry had many banks offering him innovative solutions, and it was a headache for him to choose one because all of them treated him well. At the start of our meeting, he had already made up his mind not to engage us, so he wanted to prepare us for rejection with his mooncake remark.

But the chocolate saved us! We ended up getting the deal from Henry. Our timely, thoughtful and inexpensive gift didn't win the mandate on its own, but it did foster a rapport with him that made the obstacles we faced later during the negotiation process easier to overcome. Had we believed that Henry's mooncake comment was purely a joke, or waited a few days before sending him the gift, the outcome would have been different. When you give gifts to someone — whether clients, friends or family — it helps when there's an element of surprise involved.

A Small Action Can Create Trust

Building rapport isn't just about buying gifts. A good way to establish a relationship or make a current one stronger is to win someone's trust. If you have an opportunity to do a bit of extra work for a teammate, be sure to seize it. A colleague of mine in Beijing, Ming, phoned me one Saturday because he needed some data urgently. I went to our Shanghai office, downloaded the information, and emailed it to him within an hour. I only lived five minutes from work, so this was easy for me, but Ming was still very grateful. I had cemented a trusting relationship with him, and he remembers what I did to this day.

Build Trust by Showing Dedication

When a client in Shanghai, Wesley, invited me to a dinner, I had to decline the invitation, but this ultimately strengthened our relationship. I couldn't attend because I had to stay at home to practice my Mandarin for a training session I was about to deliver for Wesley's company. As a new client, Wesley was impressed by my professionalism and thought I was very dedicated to have skipped a social event to make sure the training was a success. My small action that evening laid the platform for a trusting long-term relationship with Wesley. I still make sure to meet up with him whenever I visit Shanghai.

Take Photos at Events

If you want to start creating rapport with inspiring speakers after you've attended their events, take a photo of them on the stage (or on Zoom). Speakers can't photograph themselves, and they'll appreciate this small gesture and remember you for it. As a speaker myself, I'm definitely grateful when someone in the audience sends me a photo of me speaking.

Use Time as a Filter

Sometimes the people you want to build rapport with don't respond as enthusiastically as you'd hoped. They might be dealing with pressing issues in their lives. In cases like this, I use the passing of time to build trust. Instead of bombarding the person with successive messages shortly after we first meet, I wait for a month or two before reaching out again. Four or five messages exchanged over a year builds more trust than the same number exchanged in a week. If you're still genuinely interested in building rapport after a year, the other person will feel your sincerity and will be more likely to respond.

Make a List of Genuine Contacts

Regular but not intrusive communication helps ensure the rapport you've created with someone doesn't go stale. I keep a list of everyone I want to maintain a relationship with, and every few months I go through it and get in touch with anyone I haven't corresponded with for a while. People with integrity — who believe in me, inspire me, and have shared interests — are on the list. I don't limit it to senior professionals with big jobs. If anyone — whether a student, LinkedIn follower, or someone from a networking event — has an interesting idea, they might be included. When I'm planning a business trip, I check my list so I can meet up face to face with contacts from that city. When you're drawing up your own list, there's no need to be too precise about the benefits people will bring you because this is a long-term project and our priorities change over time. It's best to create your list simply based on who you like and trust. And always assume that the people on it will be more successful in the future than they are today.

The examples above show that even people at junior levels can do small things to build rapport. You don't need to be experienced to take a photo at a conference, buy a timely gift, or make an extra effort for a colleague. Having a good rapport with someone can pay dividends over time. Some of my clients followed me from firm to firm over the years because they trusted me to deliver what I'd promised. The stronger your relationships, the more likely that you'll be referred for jobs or business opportunities. When you meet objections (step five) and can't resolve them, go back to step two and try to build rapport and trust.

29
Thorny Issues

Every school holiday during my teenage years, I had a rendezvous with the king... of fruits. The meeting point was my aunt's fruit shop, where I'd show up just before the "king", the mighty durian, arrived by truck. I'd then help unload crates containing the spiky green fruit, which always fills the air with its unmistakable aroma, or stench, depending on your point of view. Durians are a delicacy in Southeast Asia, but their overpowering pong, which permeates through their tough outer shell, makes them an acquired taste.

For me, though, it was love at my first bite of a durian. Helping at my aunt's shop during durian season, which coincided with the school holidays in June and December, wasn't a thorn in my side — apart from the occasional prick from my favorite fruit.

Know Each Type of Customer

Besides discovering a love for durians, my fruit-shop "internship" made me see how my aunt carries out her trade. I realized that understanding customers' needs is an important skill to acquire. My aunt beats the best bankers in town. She knows her different customers inside out.

When a father shopping for his family parks his car just outside her shop, she knows he's prepared to buy plenty of fruit. Why risk getting a ticket by parking on a double-yellow line if he wants just one or two durians? She'll upsell him like the McDonald's cashier who never fails to ask, "Sir, would you like to upsize that?"

When a young man comes to the fruit shop with a girlfriend, and the couple are dressed like they're going to a party, my aunt will sell him a single durian of the highest grade (i.e. the most expensive one with the biggest margin). She recognizes that his girlfriend is too embarrassed to eat a lot, and he's too embarrassed to ask for a cheaper durian or bargain in front of his girlfriend.

When a husband and wife arrive with several large containers, my aunt realizes they want affordable durians in large numbers to make a big dessert. They're not after quality. It's a good opportunity to sell them durians that don't meet her usual standards. It may seem like she's out to rip them off, but she's actually addressing their needs.

Keeping Your Customers Happy

By knowing her customers so well and selling according to their needs, my aunt ultimately makes them happy. The father also visited a week earlier, but parked in a carpark a few hundred meters away. He could only carry four durians without breaking his arms (larger durians weigh about 2kg or more). His family got into an argument that evening because there wasn't enough of the fruit to go around. His parents-in-law visited and thought he was stingy for not buying more. But tonight, after parking next to the shop, he has more durians than his extended family can eat, and he's a happy man. Tonight, he's a loving husband and father. Tonight, he's a generous son-in-law. And it's all thanks to the durian seller who upsold him.

Meanwhile, the girlfriend of the young man is impressed. She thinks he has good taste and treats her well for buying the best single durian on offer. My aunt understands that the couple won't eat more than one durian between them. As for the "dessert king and queen" — as I'd like to call them — they're happy to be treated like royalty even though they're buying less-than-perfect fruit. Without their order, my aunt would have thrown these durians away.

First Sale of the Day

One morning, when I was sorting out durians by size, a mother with a young boy slowed down as they passed the shop. She looked at the durians and then I asked, "Do you want to try any?" She pointed at the $10/kg durians. I picked one and sniffed the bottom, but it didn't smell, so it wasn't ripe enough. After several more sniffs, I found one with a full-bodied fragrance, which signaled it was ready to be eaten.

The red needle on the weighing scale read 1.5kg. I asked, "Is $15 ok?", and the mother nodded. Fantastic, I thought, I'm about to close the sale. Most durian sellers believe that screwing up their first trade will jeopardize their entire day. Holding the durian with my left hand in a glove, I plunged my thick knife into one of the long lines that form a star shape at the bottom of the fruit. Suddenly, as I was cutting, I overheard the boy quietly saying, "I want to pee" to his mother as he tugged her hand. "We'll come back another day", the mother said to me. There went my sale.

I hoped that it wouldn't affect business for the rest of the day, so I asked my aunt how I could hedge the "pee risk". She didn't have a sales manual, but she did have some effective sales techniques. If a potential customer was a parent with a young kid, she always broke the ice with the child first. "Have you just finished school?" she'd ask. The child would nod shyly, shake their head, or stare at her silently. "Would you like a sweet?" she'd say next (because which child doesn't enjoy a treat?). I thought to myself, "Ah, that's how she hedges the pee risk — by first keeping the kid happy".

From Fruit to Finance

The ability to read people's behavior isn't just useful when selling durians; it also comes in handy when dealing with co-workers. I was having lunch on my own in my bank's pantry area, when Karen, a colleague from the legal team, came in. She took a clean cup from next to the basin, filled it with water from the dispenser, and quickly gulped down the water, seemingly wanting to rush back to her desk to work on transaction agreements. But she then took a good two minutes to wash the cup with detergent and rinse it thoroughly twice before putting it back onto the tray. After seeing all this, I decided to get to know Karen better. True enough, her work proved to be equally thorough, and her attitude toward colleagues was very considerate.

If you observe colleagues who always clear up their desk and lock their drawers before they leave for the day, you can assume they're prudent. When you want to convince them to do something, you should clearly explain the risk involved, and ensure that the risk for them is kept to a minimum.

What your colleagues say can also give you clues to their thinking beyond those provided by their behavior. Sarah works in the front office of another financial institution. She sometimes needs to seek credit approval from Craig, a senior credit risk officer, before offering loans to clients. When Sarah calls Craig, the credit officer often says, "I can't speak for long, I have a meeting with the big boss soon". Sarah feels annoyed because Craig is constantly showing off about his close relationship with the boss, an influential person within their firm.

Let's analyze Craig's behavior like a durian seller would. When someone tries to be showy in front of you, that person probably thinks highly of you. Craig wouldn't bother referring to the big boss if Sarah were a colleague at the bottom of the food chain. Moreover, Craig's good relationship with the boss is his only strong card. He hasn't achieved as much as Sarah, a well-liked salesperson who brings in plenty of revenue. Sarah becomes more tolerant of Craig when she works out why Craig has been behaving like this. Sensing Sarah's change in attitude toward him, Craig stops making the approval process so difficult.

If your colleague keeps boasting about an achievement from 10 years ago, you don't have to feel irritated or inadequate because you can safely assume that they haven't accomplished much in the last 10 years. If your colleague keeps mentioning the big companies they've worked for in the past, don't be intimidated because they're likely feeling insecure in their current job. They're afraid that you'll look down on them, and their defense mechanism has kicked in without them knowing.

But if a colleague says to you, "I see you as part of the team", be careful. You may have met a rival who is strong in office politics. One way to defend yourself from politics is to have a "partner in crime" in the company. It's more difficult for politically motivated colleagues to attack you when you have a buddy to watch your back. Next time you're having thorny issues with unpleasant co-workers, put on the gloves of the durian seller and try to analyze their behavior and their needs. What are they trying to cover up?

30

Offer Free Samples

Jewel is a spectacular shopping and dining venue in Singapore's Changi Airport that looks like a giant gemstone if viewed from afar. But it's when you step inside the greenhouse-like structure that it really starts to dazzle you. The shops are set amongst lush terraces, containing more than 200 plant species, and are centered around the Rain Vortex, the world's tallest indoor waterfall, which harvests rainwater and sends it cascading down 40 meters from an inverted-dome roof.

I visited Jewel soon after it opened. After spending time admiring the vortex, I noticed a long queue outside an ice cream store. A lovely aroma was filling the air because the ice cream cones were being made right on the spot, but this wasn't the reason that so many people were lining up. The ice cream was a hit because customers were trying it before buying it. The shop wasn't just allowing you to sample its products if you asked politely; offering free tasters had become standard practice, even when people already knew the type of ice cream they wanted to order.

Employees were preparing wooden sample sticks in advance to make it as easy as possible to taste the various exotic flavors and to ensure nobody felt shy about taking the free ice cream. This small action made good business sense because it encouraged customers to come back in the future to try more varieties. Visitors to Jewel could see that the company must have good products, otherwise it wouldn't be confident enough to give out freebies before people parted with their money.

Offering free samples also makes sense for us as individuals, as I've found out during my career.

A Free Ride Into Teaching

At the start of my teaching career, I spent three years speaking free of charge — first about financial engineering and then about corporate risk advisory — at a university in Singapore. I was a vice president at a U.S. bank and knew the subject matter well, but I didn't have any teaching credentials. If I'd demanded even a small fee I couldn't have got the gig. The professor would have been burdened with more administrative work had I been paid, and would have faced hurdles seeking internal approval, so I made life easier for him by offering a freebie (me!). I was also too shy to mention the subject of pay and I didn't know if I was good enough to be a teacher. But I had already become interested in training young people, so the financial rewards weren't important — it was an honor to be invited to lecture at a leading university.

My small action of deciding against asking for money not only secured me this first job, it set me up for a rewarding career as a lecturer in several tertiary institutions later on. When I moved to Shanghai, I kept on teaching in Singapore and the university started paying my travel costs. But that was only after the previous students said they enjoyed my classes and the professor was happy with my work. With some experience and good feedback under my belt, it was more straightforward for the professor to justify paying me. These days, when friends tell me that they'd love to teach and then ask what the pay is like, I advise them to consider initially doing it for free to secure their first teaching gig.

To Split Revenue or Not

While I was working in fixed income at a large investment bank, I helped the manager in charge of equity to sell his products. I didn't immediately ask how we would split the revenue or if my annual bonus would be increased. It was more important to learn about equity transactions, prove I could work on that side of the business, and help close a few deals for the bank. My strategy of not focusing on my own short-term financial gain turned out to be correct. When this first deal was successfully completed, the manager said he was happy for me to market his products to a much wider client base. Selling his products accelerated my learning in a new area of banking far more effectively than if I'd done a training course. If you're given an opportunity to take on a new responsibility at work, focus on how it could benefit your career and skills in the future. Don't worry about your salary in the short term because when you bring enough value to your business, your pay or bonus will increase, otherwise your company risks losing you to competitors.

How Debbie Got Her Dream Job

When I worked in risk management, my team employed a young trainee called Debbie. After going through the bank's training program and doing short-term rotational stints in several departments, Debbie had been assigned to us in a full-time role. But she didn't want to be in risk management; she had great communication skills and felt she was better suited to a front-office position.

Debbie never gave up on her dream. She volunteered to come in at 7am every day to work for free in the front office (checking over trades from the previous day), before starting in my team at 9am. The quality of her work for both parts of the bank was excellent, and everyone was delighted when Debbie secured her sought-after transfer to the trading desk about a year later. Working for free is a difficult decision to make, but it paid off for Debbie because it changed her career and her life. People sometimes think they can just wait and hope for a big break like an internal transfer to crop up. But hope isn't a strategy; offering freebies is.

Doing some of your work free of charge — whether for your employer or by following your interests outside the office — rarely brings you immediate career advancement, but it can create opportunities over the long term. Just remember that you won't be asked to sacrifice your time; you'll have to proactively seek out new tasks and pitch your ideas, like Debbie did with her plan to do an extra shift each morning.

By giving up your time now without financial recognition, you can reap rewards later on. The next time you pass an ice cream shop offering free samples, you'll understand this strategy and how it could apply to your career. The goodwill the shop has generated to keep you coming back again and again is far more valuable than the free ice cream.

31

One Eye on the CEO, Another on the CFO

I occasionally run training sessions for mid-level professionals who are being groomed for senior jobs at their companies. I like to kick off these events with an unusual icebreaker.

People in the group all pair up with someone they don't know. I ask them to exchange three personal items — such as a purse, watch, ring, notebook, or bag — and take a couple of minutes to study their partner's objects. Then I get them to make some general assumptions about the other person based on what they've just looked at. I hear comments such as "well organized", "trendy", "practical", "family guy", "colorful"… the list goes on. If someone hands over a dog-eared old wallet alongside two expensive new things, it's likely the wallet was a gift from a loved one, so that person might be characterized as sentimental for keeping it so long. People who have an umbrella with them on a sunny day might be cautious in nature. Those with high-end phones and gadgets probably enjoy staying abreast with the latest technology trends.

When I ask the participants what they think of the observations they've just heard about themselves, they actually agree with them most of the time. While this short exercise doesn't provide perfect insights, it does demonstrate what can be achieved by the small action of opening your eyes and observing. You can learn important things about people more quickly, and use this as a base for an in-depth relationship.

Facial Recognition

Instead of looking down at my phone when I'm out walking, I like to scan the street for familiar faces. You'd be surprised how many people you come across if you do this, including those you haven't seen for a while. I was crossing the road in Canary Wharf, one of London's financial districts, when I spotted Nick, a former colleague who I hadn't met for 15 years. We had a chat on the sidewalk. It was so good to bump into an old friend.

I do a similar thing on airplanes. When I travel from Beijing to Hong Kong, I typically take the Friday 6pm flight. It's a popular option with Hong Kong business people who've just spent the week in the Chinese capital and are on their way home for the weekend, so there's always a good chance of seeing someone I know. I look out for ex-colleagues, clients and other familiar faces on both sides of the aisle as I board the plane. If you've been trying unsuccessfully to book an appointment with a client, a four-hour flight is a perfect opportunity to talk to them. You have a captive audience. Even a fierce business competitor could one day become a partner or a colleague. They'll appreciate it if you acknowledge them, and a short mid-air conversation could form the beginning of a beneficial relationship.

By keeping your eyes open on a street or a plane or wherever you happen to be, you'll gain networking opportunities that would otherwise have passed you by.

My Ears Saved My First Job

My first job in banking was in FX sales, and my core task was to answer calls from clients who wanted to execute currency transactions. While FX trades are executed over electronic platforms these days, our processes were still pretty manual back then. I sat on the trading floor, and on my desk was a large panel of red LED lights that flashed when phone calls came in. The lights on the top two rows were the most important. They were called hotlines. When one of them started flashing, I had to press it immediately because it would be a call from a large public sector or multinational corporate client. If a client wanted to buy US$50m worth of Japanese yen, for example, I'd have to shout out to the yen FX trader through a voice box. The conversation would go something like this:

"Dollar-yen in fifty," I say. (We don't add the "million" part because it's obvious.)

"20/22," replies the trader. (This means the price is 108.20, if the client is selling; or 108.22, if the client is buying. We both already know the big figure, 108, so only the numbers after the decimal point are communicated.)

Immediately, I relay the "22" buy price to the client, and check if they want to go ahead. If they agree with the price, I shout, "mine at 22!"

Then the trader confirms the trade has been executed: "done at 22!"

But trades didn't always go so smoothly in those days. Sometimes clients could take more than a few seconds to decide whether to buy (or to "hit" me, in dealing-room lingo), during which time the price would have moved. While I was on the phone speaking with a client, I was also listening out for the trader shouting "off", which signaled a change in the price. Whenever I heard this, I had to tell the client straight away, before they decided to hit me. If I wasn't quick enough, I could lose money for the bank. If the price increased to 23 in the above transaction, that would be a $5,000 loss. All this happened within seconds. I had to constantly keep my ears open — one on the client, the other on the trader — in a highly pressurized environment.

Being thrown into the deep end of the trading floor was an early lesson in the value of listening. No matter what role you're in, it's critical to pay close attention to what those around you are saying, especially when your work gets intense. Your listening skills can help you identify the priorities of the people you work with.

Learn How to Multitask

Don't let people tell you you can't multitask. You can, if you're trained for it. If you've ever been to a large international conference, you might have seen translators sitting in a corner booth and translating a speaker's presentations into another language for attendees who listen in via headsets.

These highly skilled simultaneous translators listen and speak almost in real time. I saw one up close when I brought my bank's head of mergers and acquisitions (M&A), an experienced British banker, to see my client, the chief executive of a large Chinese company. We had a potential M&A transaction to discuss.

My colleague couldn't speak Mandarin, while my client preferred not to converse in English. If I were to do the translation myself, it would double our meeting time and affect the flow of the discussion. Fortunately, the Chinese CEO had a personal assistant, Aubrey, who could do simultaneous translations. She sat just behind him. As she listened to my British colleague, Aubrey translated softly into Mandarin via a microphone and the CEO heard her voice in his earpiece. Thanks to Aubrey's flawless multitasking abilities, my colleague and client spoke in different languages about a large acquisition with virtually no time lag.

These skills don't come overnight. China has schools that train simultaneous translators, and some of their exercises involve teaching the brain to multitask. In one example I know of, the instructor has a conversation with students as they walk up a flight of stairs. The teacher then suddenly stops and asks the students how many steps they've just climbed, which forces the aspiring translators to converse and count at the same time. This isn't just a test of their language skills; it also reinforces their ability to multitask, which is essential for a successful career as a simultaneous translator.

I'm not as skilled as a translator, but I still had to multitask at work. If I was on the phone and a new team member was speaking to a client at the same time, I had to stay engaged in my own conversation while also paying attention to what the new recruit was saying. If they overpromised or gave clients wrong information, I'd have to intervene. Developing your own ability to multitask will enable you to take on more responsibilities in your career.

Make Full Use of Both Your Eyes and Ears

Is it possible to open your eyes and ears to several things while still focusing on your primary task? Yes. When you go into a meeting with two important people from a company — the CEO and CFO, for example — you should have your eyes on both of them. The CEO will probably do most of the talking, but you can't ignore the CFO. Observe their body language and look for clues about whether they're agreeing or disagreeing with what their boss is saying. Keep one eye on the CEO, another on the CFO... and one ear on your colleague, who may want to jump into the discussion while you're speaking.

In larger meetings, many people focus on the narrow dialogue between themselves and the most senior person. But this means missing out on potentially crucial nuances in the group discussion. Next time you're in a meeting, try to also observe the subtle body language of those not speaking: keep your eyes and ears open to everyone. The person with the biggest title may not be the ultimate decision maker or the one with the most influence.

There's a lot you can gain by being observant, both by watching people carefully and listening to them with curiosity. Most importantly of all, being a good observer helps you build fruitful business relationships externally and internally.

Part Six

Life's Never Perfect:
Coping With the Challenges

32

SY's Challenge

As a fan of modern architecture, I've long admired One Raffles Place in Singapore. This 60-story skyscraper in the heart of the central business district is one of the city's tallest buildings. In my mind, it's also one of the most beautiful. Designed by the late, great Japanese architect Kenzo Tange — whose accomplishments include winning the prestigious Pritzker Architecture Prize — the tower was completed back in 1986 and consists of two dramatic triangular structures. From certain angles, it looks like a flat piece of cardboard. From other angles, it looks like a knife.

I was passing by one day and I had the urge to touch one of the edges of this landmark high-rise. I was curious to know how it felt because Tange had managed to make the edges look so sharp from afar. As I approached One Raffles Place, I noticed a young woman who was trying to catch the attention of passersby. She wasn't in business attire, but wore blue jeans and a casual grey top. She had a badge hanging around her neck and was holding a clipboard. She was clearly trying to sell something, but most people were doing their best to avoid eye contact with her, let alone talk to her.

Suddenly I was more curious about her than the building. In today's digital world, why would anyone want to sell things on the street, especially without an elaborate stand? I went up to the woman to find out what she was selling, and why she wasn't doing it online to reach a more engaged audience. Introducing herself as SY, she told me she was asking for donations on behalf of a charity that offers free medicine to elderly people who are struggling to afford healthcare.

She said digital marketing may make us sympathize with the plight of these people, but it's unlikely to make us reach for our wallets. Face-to-face marketing is still the most effective method for getting charitable contributions, SY added. It's a numbers game: on average about one in 100 people will donate, so if she aims to have 10 donations, she needs to ask 1,000 passersby.

For me, the odds still seemed stacked against SY: she was only talking about a 1% success rate. So I also asked SY how she stays motivated when many people avoid her like fish trying to escape a shark. Most of us face a few rejections each week in our jobs; SY encounters hundreds every day. How does she manage to keep a genuine smile on her face?

SY admitted that constant rejection is the main challenge of her role. However, when someone does donate, she knows that the money will go to old folks in need. This makes her happy and gives her a feeling of purpose in her job. SY then went on to say, "*when your purpose is greater than your challenge, you can overcome your challenge*".

I was blown away by this statement, especially coming from someone who'd only recently graduated from university. I was touched by her strong sense of purpose. I reached for my wallet and donated some money to the charity.

I also realized that her attitude to her working life has a wider applicability. In my own life, the key challenge is trying to juggle the many things I want to do, such as writing my LinkedIn blog, teaching at universities, coaching students and professionals, delivering high-quality webinars, traveling around the world to speak, and spending time with family and friends. My schedule is packed from Monday to Sunday, so there's little time left for myself. But whenever I receive messages from people about how my work has made a positive impact on their lives, I feel fulfilled and rewarded.

You're bound to face challenges in your work. When they become too big to handle, try to think of a bigger purpose that can help motivate you.

33

Pure Profit

If you jump into a taxi in Singapore or Hong Kong and ask the driver how their day is going, many will reply "yet to cover my costs!" They're talking about the costs of petrol and renting their car, which they must pay every day regardless of how many passengers they pick up. It often takes drivers a few hours for their fare income to pay for their daily expenses. But any rides they do after they reach this mark are "pure profit" in their minds.

We're not taught to think in this way in accounting or math classes at school, where we focus on calculating profit using averages. The textbook way to work out taxi drivers' profit is to subtract their average cost per km from their average fare per km. Using this method, drivers generate profit from the start of their shift. They could quit work early and still make a profit… but could they really?

In the real world, cab drivers have no practical use for average profit calculations. Taxi companies charge them rent for a full day, so they'll lose money if they stop driving too soon. Drivers are motivated by their belief in pure profit. They'll sometimes go hungry and hold the call of nature for hours so they can keep driving until they reach the point at which their daily expenses are met. The money they receive from customers after that is theirs to keep.

Is this taxi-driver way of thinking too simplistic to apply elsewhere? No, in fact, it's a relevant concept in many other walks of life.

When you order a meal at any fast-food chain, the server almost always asks you whether you'd like to upsize your meal. Don't underestimate the power of this small action. Like any business, fast-food restaurants have to pay staff, inventory, marketing, rental and other costs. If you only buy a simple burger or a small meal, chances are that much of your money is going toward paying these expenses. But if you upsize, the extra $1 or so that you're spending is almost pure profit for their business. It costs hardly anything and requires very little effort for the staff to add extra fries, or pour more soft drink.

The idea of pure profit can even apply in the world of banking. At the start of the fourth quarter one year, the head of investment banking for APAC at my firm called a meeting of all the managing directors to tell us that we had to work especially hard for the next three months. He said during the first half of the year our revenue paid for our salary, travel, technology, office-rental, and support-staff costs. The revenue we were about to generate in the final quarter would largely determine how big our bonuses (i.e. our pure profit) would be for the year.

Our boss didn't want us to relax and think that our bonus numbers had already been set in stone. He made it clear that if we didn't bring in business late in the year, there would be little in terms of bonuses because our revenue thus far had only covered our costs. As he spoke, I couldn't help thinking of the cab drivers lining up their red taxis at the stand below our office in central Hong Kong. They would be focused on the pure profit they would be making later on in their shifts. The head of investment banking was using the same simple concept to encourage us to keep working hard until the year was over.

I don't always think of pure profit in a financial sense. My exercise regime often includes going for a run, whether on the street or on a treadmill at the gym. The first 15 to 20 minutes of the jog cover my "costs" (i.e. the effort of getting warmed up). The fitness benefits aren't that great. After covering these costs, I believe that every minute I run is pure profit: it's making me fitter rather than just maintaining my current fitness levels. I usually set myself a target to run for 30 minutes, but always convince myself to run a few more minutes after hitting that initial goal because I've already changed into my exercise gear and warmed up. These days I rarely quit my runs too soon.

Any time you face challenges in your career or in life, think about the effort you've made to get where you are and remember that if you put in a bit more work, you can reach the pure-profit stage. For example, when you've invested time trying to establish a business relationship, don't stop if the initial contact has been unsuccessful. It may take just one more phone call to make that person a high quality connection. When you've picked up the basics of a new language and have since plateaued, push yourself to practice a little more to take advantage of what you've already learned in class.

Try not to waste the time you've invested in something. Pure profit could be just around the corner, if you persevere like a taxi driver who stays on the road for those final few lucrative rides. We don't learn about pure profit at school and our companies don't use it to calculate their financial results, but when we want to motivate ourselves to achieve something special, it's a valuable tool to use. The next time you see me jogging and ask me how my run is going, I'm likely to reply, "yet to cover my costs!"

34

Food or Service?

When I teach at university, I often invite colleagues, clients and other senior people I know to talk to my students. Alvin, the CEO of a US$7 billion real estate fund (whom I first mentioned in Chapter 5) once spoke to a class of mine about what he looks out for when he hires people. One piece of advice really stood out from his presentation. He told the audience that, "it's better to be honest than to be impressive" during job interviews. This runs counter to the usual thinking that we must do all we can to dazzle the people who are considering whether to offer us a job.

One of my students told Alvin that she felt under pressure to impress interviewers because competition for jobs is so intense. There's a risk, however, that we oversell our skills and abilities as we try to impress hiring managers and outshine our rivals to secure a coveted position. We may even avoid telling the truth and say we're better at something than we really are. This can have serious repercussions when we start work because we may not live up to our employer's expectations.

It's better to be honest when asked if you can perform a particular task or have expertise in a particular area. The company may still hire you, but you've managed expectations and your boss knows in advance that you need additional training. Or perhaps you won't get a job offer, but at least you won't be stuck in a role that wasn't right for you in the first place. When Alvin's talk was over, I looked back on my career and asked myself whether I'd ever benefited from being honest rather than impressive in an interview. One incident immediately sprung to mind.

After graduating from university, I was keen to see the world and experience other countries and cultures, but I didn't have much money. So I thought the best way to travel extensively would be to work as a flight attendant. An airline was advertising jobs and I went to a hotel for an initial walk-in interview. As one of our tasks, we were given a passage to read out to make sure our English was up to scratch. There was one word ("expedite") that I didn't know how to say properly, but fortunately my friend, who was doing the same test, told me the correct pronunciation. I passed the first round.

I then went to the airline's training center for the next stage of the recruitment process. There were more than 100 hopeful candidates. We broke off into groups of 10 and were instructed to play some board games. People who tried to dominate the discussions or who kept quiet the whole time didn't do so well. When the games were over, the interviewer called out two names, one of which was mine. We stayed on. The other eight people in my group were told, "you may leave now".

All the selected candidates from each group then went to the swimming pool within the training complex. We had to swim 50 meters to prove our ability to stay buoyant in the event of a plane landing on water. I wasn't a good swimmer, but I passed. I felt relieved and happy. The thought that I would soon be flying around to see the world thrilled me. We left the pool area, got changed, and met up again for tea and coffee. Our host was a senior manager from the airline, a tall middle-aged man who exuded authority. We were sipping our drinks and casually chatting when he asked us, "what do you think is more important: service or food?" Without missing a beat, I put up my hand and replied, "food is more important". He said, "you may leave now!"

I'm joking; he didn't throw me out right away. But two weeks later I received a rejection letter, and my poor answer to his question was the reason I think I fell at the final hurdle. The interviewer, of course, wanted to hear that service is the priority for a premium airline, or that food and service are equally important. If I'd paused to think about how to impress him, I may not have said food. For me as a young man, however, food was the most honest answer. Up until that time, I had dined out mainly at hawker centers, which serve street food in Singapore. I would always choose where to eat purely based on the food. I neither valued nor had much experience of good service.

The airline and I benefited from me giving an authentic rather than an impressive answer. Although I really wanted to travel and was initially attracted by the cabin-crew job, I wasn't a service-oriented person back then and I would have been unhappy in the role. I would have delivered hawker-center service to passengers, which would have been bad for the company and draining for me.

Missing out on a position because of your honesty during an interview can make you feel disappointed in the short term, but it's likely to work out for the best over the long run. When you're not true to yourself, you set yourself up for unnecessary challenges on the job. I'd like to thank the interviewer for rejecting me. He knew I wasn't a good fit and wouldn't have lasted more than a year in the sky!

35

Why Reveal Failures

Twenty one years ago I applied for a PhD program in operational research and financial engineering at Princeton University. I'd been working for a few years by then, but had developed a strong interest in teaching and research. Operational research and financial engineering — which solves financial problems using mathematical techniques — was an exciting, emerging field at that time and was a passion of mine. I also aspired to attend a prestigious Ivy League school and eventually work full-time as an academic. The Princeton program seemed perfectly matched to my ambitions and I was all set to uproot my life to achieve them.

A few months after applying, I received a letter from Princeton. As I opened it, I looked for the word "unfortunately" and hoped that I wouldn't see it... but I did. "Unfortunately" was there staring right back at me. I was devastated! I'd been planning to quit my job, move to a new country, and spend the next four to five years getting a PhD. But my dream of becoming an academic was shattered in an instant.

Dear Mr Sim,
Your application for admission to Princeton University has been received in the Graduate School and by the appropriate academic department. Unfortunately, we cannot offer you admission at this time. Your application, however, suggests that you could do well as a graduate student, and we would like to reserve a final decision until a later time. We have therefore placed your name on a waiting list.

Now, 21 years later, I'm still waiting!

This isn't the first time I've mentioned my Princeton disappointment. I've also revealed it in my bio and visual CV (see next page). I believe there are four main benefits of disclosing some of your own failures and weaknesses.

You Become More Trustworthy

Revealing a failure or weakness shows you're being authentic about yourself. People will trust you more because you've been honest with them. Trust is the most important factor when developing relationships and doing business. When people trust you, they're more likely to want to work with you.

You Stand Out

Most people only show the best parts of their lives on social media — from holiday photos to work promotions — so sharing a failure or weakness on LinkedIn or another platform will help your post stand out from the rest. Your connections will find it refreshing to read the occasional story about something that's gone wrong. But remember to only mention failures that you're comfortable being made public.

You Become Easier to Relate to

When you talk about a weakness or failure, you become more likeable and more human. Everyone has faults of their own, so people will identify and empathize with you after hearing about yours. Instead of envying your boastful social posts, your connections will root for you, refer opportunities your way, and may even offer you tips about overcoming your weakness.

You Accept Who You Are

Revealing a failure or weakness means you accept that particular part of yourself. You then either learn to live with it, or take action to change it. Being open about your shortcomings can give you a tremendous sense of relief because it removes the pressure to be perfect all the time. The worst thing you can do is deny a weakness and pretend to be someone you're not. But bear in mind, if it's a wound that you are still recovering from, you may want to wait a while before revealing more. If it's a scar (a cut that has healed), it may look ugly, but discussing it can help you accept who you are.

Revealing Failure at Job Interviews

Job interviews provide a good platform to disclose failures and weaknesses, and you'll likely be asked questions to prompt you. Avoid banal replies — such as "I work too hard", "I'm a perfectionist", or "I don't know when to stop" — because these simply try to disguise strengths as weaknesses. Smart hiring managers will see through this kind of trickery in an instant. You should instead provide a genuine example of a failure you've experienced in your career or life. You can then talk about how you accepted it and learned from it, or ultimately overcame it, or are still working on it. Whatever stage you're at, be sure to tell the interviewer how the failure has made you a stronger person. Showcasing a weakness will also set you up for success when you start the job because your manager won't expect you to immediately perform well in that area and will provide training and support to help you improve.

Karl, a Hong Kong-based MBA student of mine, secured a job interview in the Singapore office of a big private equity fund with more than US$100 billion in assets under management. He asked me to help prepare him for the interview, but I had a packed schedule on the day he planned to arrive. When Karl landed in Singapore, he took a taxi from Changi airport to my apartment, dropped off his luggage and went straight to… my hairdresser, where I was having a haircut ahead of a presentation I was making. Karl sat on the barber's chair beside me as I gave him a mock interview.

We agreed that Karl's main weakness is his verbal communication skills. He doesn't express himself as articulately as most professionals in client-facing jobs. I told Karl that he should be open about his oral presentation abilities because they would soon become obvious to the interviewer. He should then explain how he overcomes his limitations and maintains strong relationships with his clients in other ways. In the actual interview, Karl said he sometimes struggles when he first meets a new client, but he builds trust by delivering excellent work, keeping in regular contact, and occasionally buying small, thoughtful gifts for them. He got the job!

When I sold complex derivatives products during my early days in structured product sales, I always revealed their drawbacks and potential risks to my clients. Clients trust you more if you disclose the downside risk. The same concept applies to our lives and careers. Our personal weaknesses are just as important as our strengths when we're interviewing for a role, dealing with colleagues, or posting on social media. Try to find an opportunity to talk about one of your own failures. Admitting you're no good at something is the first step if you eventually want to overcome your weakness in that area, and if you want other people to support you along the way.

CAREER PATH
What my CV looks like

Managing Director,
UBS Investment Bank

Director, Citi

Risk Manager, Stan Chart

FX Sales, DBS Bank

B. Engineering, NUS

What I have been through

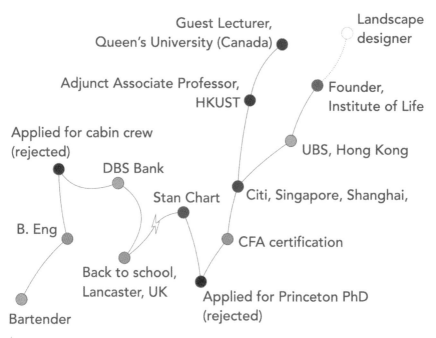

Guest Lecturer,
Queen's University (Canada)

Landscape
designer

Adjunct Associate Professor,
HKUST

Founder,
Institute of Life

Applied for cabin crew
(rejected)

UBS, Hong Kong

DBS Bank

Stan Chart

Citi, Singapore, Shanghai,

B. Eng

CFA certification

Back to school,
Lancaster, UK

Applied for Princeton PhD
(rejected)

Bartender

⚡ *Asian financial crisis*

149

36

The Same-Bowl Rule

When someone watches you closely to ensure you're doing your job properly, it can be an unpleasant and overbearing experience. Perhaps your boss is an obsessive micro manager, or perhaps your team is tightly monitored by an industry regulator to ensure you follow strict compliance policies. But there's one thing that's even more challenging than being scrutinized too much: working on your own with nobody looking over your shoulder.

My father was a hawker (street food vendor) in Singapore for over 30 years, and his tiny stall sold a single dish: prawn noodle soup. Every morning, he cooked a big vat of broth using prawn shells, pork bones, garlic — which he roasted in caramelized rock sugar — and soy sauce. He added sliced prawns and lean pork when he served up bowls of this delicious concoction. From elementary school until my university days, I helped out my father at his business every Sunday and during holidays. It was hot and hard work. As a teenager, I hated getting up early to be at the hawker stall by 7.30am, and I never got used to my hands always smelling of prawn! One of my main duties was dishwashing. We only had one small sink with running water, and that was near the cooking station and was used for cleaning our utensils and hands. For dishes, we used a three-pail system.

The first pail was deep and filled with soapy water, so customers' dirty bowls and cutlery would be left soaking in it for a while. Following the soak, I cleaned each bowl with a sponge, before dunking it into a second bucket containing clean water to wash off most of the soap. Next came a final rinse in the third pail. Then I drained the water out of the bowls, so they were ready to use again. After I washed about 50 to 60 bowls, the water in the second bucket turned murky and I changed it.

When I reached my senior year in high school, about a year before I went into the army for national service, my father let me cook noodles for customers. One time, as we were about to close the stall for the day, I made lunch for myself. I stepped into the sauna-hot cooking station where steam was constantly rising from the boiling noodle water. I took one of our "rooster bowls" — a traditional Chinese design featuring a black and red rooster — from the clean stack of dishes and rinsed it again under running water before putting in my noodles. My father caught me rinsing the bowl. "Don't wash it a second time," he told me sternly but softly, to avoid alerting any customers. I froze, forgetting my meal as I tried to think of some words to pacify him. But I wasn't quite sure why what I'd done was wrong. Seeing the blank look on my face, my father said, "if the bowl is clean enough for customers, it's clean enough for you".

I'd washed the bowl again because in other eateries I'd sometimes been served bowls with a tiny bit of food stuck to the side. Have you experienced that yourself? I didn't trust my own bucket-cleaning skills. But in doing so I'd undermined my father and the three-pail method that he'd been using effectively for so many years. If a customer had suddenly come to our stall and seen me, they would have doubted the cleanliness of our bowls.

After receiving my father's advice, I put more effort into my dishwashing, and I decided to never give my own bowl an extra rinse. Even if I were alone in the hawker stall, I'd always eat from the same bowls washed in the same way as my customers' ones. I learned an important lesson about work ethics that day: do the right thing even when no one else is watching. This isn't easy because it's tempting to take shortcuts on the job, but in my experience people who bend the rules will ultimately be caught out by their company or by industry regulators.

This same-bowl rule followed me from the hawker stand into my banking career. I made sure the financial products I sold to clients were those that I'd have bought myself. This might have cost me some business in the short term, but I knew I would eventually benefit from the trust it created between me and my clients.

37

Can You Pass the Airport Test?

I invited Dan, a campus recruiter at a tier-one bank, to come over to my Institute of Life office at Cyberport in Hong Kong. He knew I did a lot of work to train students and young professionals, and we were keen to exchange ideas. Dan told me that selecting young people to hire was always difficult because the candidates had excellent grades and were technically proficient.

So I asked what helps set job seekers apart. He said that when assessing someone during an interview, he thinks about what it would be like to be trapped with that person at an airport for three hours because of a flight delay during a business trip. Would they be good company and be an engaging conversationalist when the work-related chat runs out and the talk turns to more personal topics? This "airport test" may seem like a narrow scenario because many jobs don't involve plane travel, but it has a wider applicability. You probably spend more of your waking hours with your colleagues than with your partner. It's not surprising that recruiters and line managers like to hire a diverse range of people, who they think will be interesting and enjoyable to work with, both inside and outside the office.

While a hiring manager won't ever mention the airport test to you directly, they will infer your ability to pass it through the stories you tell during the interview. Obvious opportunities for storytelling will crop up in questions that begin with "tell us about a time when...", but you should try to include brief stories in some of your other answers. If you're asked about your personal interests, for example, don't just list them; use stories to bring them to life.

People, including hiring managers, will remember your stories better than they remember the raw facts about you. It's important to prepare several good stories in your mind, so you have them on tap to help you hold down a conversation with a wide variety of people. Stories aren't only critical during interviews and when socializing with colleagues; they're also valuable when networking and meeting clients. People from diverse backgrounds often have the ability to tell great stories because they have a range of unique and interesting life experiences to draw on. So don't hold back on your stories just because your background differs from that of the interviewer. Employers increasingly want to hire people who can provide valuable diversity of thought to enhance the productivity of their teams.

What makes a good story? The three basic elements are setting (where and when the event took place), conflict (a problem or challenge), and resolution (a solution or happy ending). Once you establish these components, you have a complete story that can be told to suit multiple purposes. Let me give you an example.

Getting on Stage for the First Time

On my high school report card, which I've kept to this day, my teacher described me as "soft-spoken and timid", and suggested that I "should learn to mix freely". Several years later, when I was studying for my engineering degree, I decided to address these issues, and also overcome my stage fright in front of large groups. I asked Peter, the choreographer of a university dance group, if I could appear in his next event. Knowing that I had no dance experience, he hesitated.

"Can you dance, Eric?"
"Not really, but I'll be happy just standing behind the dancers."
"Will you carry an umbrella?"
"I'll carry whatever props you ask me to, Peter."

"Ok, you're in."

The small action of playing a minor role in the dance production succeeded in making me more confident, and this confidence ultimately led to me becoming a teacher and public speaker, although not until many years later.

In this story, the setting is my school days from high school until university, the problem is my timid nature and fear of being in front of an audience, and the solution is getting involved in the dance group. Like most stories, the beauty of this one is that it can be deployed to illustrate a variety of points. I sometimes talk about joining the dance group to show how I overcame a weakness. But equally, I use it to highlight the value of patience and perseverance because it took me so many years to overcome my stage fright. It's also a good anecdote to highlight that I'm happy to take baby steps at the beginning when learning a new skill. And if an interviewer ever asks me about a time I went out of my comfort zone, this would be a great example.

One Story, Many Reasons to Tell it

Let's pause and do a brief exercise. First, think of a story from your life that can be easily told in a few minutes and has a setting, conflict and resolution. Second, brainstorm some keywords and phrases that immediately spring to mind from the story (e.g. "patience", "leadership", and "overcoming challenges"). Then expand all or some of these keywords into a list of potential applications for the story. For example, I could use the dance-group story to demonstrate the leadership qualities I admire, highlighting how Peter took a chance on me and didn't brush my request aside. Each time you tell a story, make sure to have a clear reason in your mind for telling it. If you go through this exercise, you'll soon work out multiple reasons to deploy the same story to answer different questions.

Storytelling doesn't just make you more interesting in the eyes of others; it's a good way of building internal resilience. Before you face your next big challenge, prepare yourself by thinking about how you've overcome obstacles in the past. Tell these success stories to your family and friends. Retelling stories on a regular basis can reinforce a sense of confidence, and make the difficulties you face seem less daunting. Confidence comes from an accumulation of small successes!

Part Seven

Leaps of Faith: Why It Pays to Take Risks

38
A Leap of Faith

Gao was my MSc in Financial Mathematics classmate 20 years ago. He enjoyed the subject so much that he went on to get a PhD in it. I wasn't so keen on the MSc. A few months into the course, I realized that my travel schedule was making it difficult to attend classes, and that proving the Black Scholes option-pricing model wasn't very helpful in my day job. I preferred the practical side of finance to stochastic calculus. I quit the master's course.

Gao recently reminded me that when he first graduated with his PhD, I got him a job interview with the American bank I was working with. He didn't end up taking that role because he was highly sought after by many other firms, and he has since built a successful career in risk management at a global bank. Anyway, Gao was grateful for my help back then and we've kept in touch ever since.

One day, Gao asked if I'd provide some career advice to his intern, Sam, who'd been working for a year in the Singapore office of his bank. Sam's postgraduate internship as a model validation quant, a middle-office role, was drawing to a close. He wanted a permanent position in risk or the front office. Gao didn't have any headcount to hire. Sam was growing anxious because he couldn't find any suitable jobs in any bank in Singapore, no matter how hard he tried.

I was based in Hong Kong at the time, so I had a video call with Sam. I could tell from this chat that he was an intelligent and diligent worker with an excellent attitude. His academic background was exceptional: he had a degree in financial mathematics from one of France's prestigious *grandes écoles*. But like many fresh graduates, he wasn't sure what to do to kickstart his career in the financial industry.

"Are you open to roles in Hong Kong?" I asked Sam.
"Yes, I am," he replied.
"Look, I don't have a position for you, but I suggest you fly to Hong Kong and meet people. I can introduce you to a few people when you're here."

Then there was a long silence. I could tell he was wondering whether to bother traveling about 1,600 miles just to try his luck in the hope he might meet someone who could get him a role. "Not all the jobs available in Hong Kong will be advertised, so if you come here and meet people in person, it will definitely give you an advantage," I explained to Sam. "and even if you don't receive a job offer right away, you'll get to see what Hong Kong is like and you'll network with people who could help you in the future."

We ended the call without a concrete plan, but later that day Sam told me he'd booked his flight to Hong Kong. The words "meet people" had resounded in his mind. After arranging his travel, he told a friend on the trading floor at his bank in Singapore that he was flying to Hong Kong on a personal visit, and hoped to go to the Hong Kong office to discuss opportunities. His friend immediately gave him several contacts there, and Sam sent out emails expressing a strong interest to meet them.

Before Sam left for Hong Kong, three people in the bank's trading team agreed to see him, although they had no jobs officially on offer. Sam arrived in the city on a Wednesday and had his meetings over two days. On Friday night, he came to one of my networking events and told me that he'd made a great impression on the people he'd met. He flew back to Singapore over the weekend, and on Monday he was offered his dream job — trading equities at one of the best equity houses in the market.

When Sam paid for his trip, a costly outlay for a young intern, it was an act of faith. This small action had a snowball effect. It led to him talking to his friend, which got him the meetings and eventually the job. If Sam had been more cautious, the outcome might have been different. If he'd tried to confirm his meetings before making his booking, the managers might have turned down his request, so as not to encourage an intern to pay for all that expensive travel when no jobs had been advertised. But Sam took the pressure off them by saying he was already coming to Hong Kong on a personal trip, and he simply asked for 30 minutes of their time over coffee with no strings attached.

My "meet people" advice didn't get Sam the job; his own determination did. Booking a visit to Hong Kong before he'd even lined up any meetings led to his success. Sam told me, "I'm glad I took that leap of faith!"

You're probably thinking that Sam was lucky to have received advice from me, a senior professional. The truth is that Sam is just one of the many people I've given advice and opportunities to. But not everyone recognizes the value of these opportunities and still fewer people successfully grab them. As a reader of this book, you've already taken a step to help improve yourself. After finishing this chapter, you could write a LinkedIn or Instagram post about the lessons you've learned so far. You could tag Institute of Life or add hashtag #66smallactions in the post. We might then notice your post and invite you to one of our events. Your success isn't guaranteed, just like it wasn't for Sam when he bought the plane ticket. Will you take a leap of faith?

39

Why Take Risks?

Entrepreneurs aren't the only ones taking risks in their careers; employees need to take some risks too.

Taking My First Risk

Two years after I started working in banking I decided that I wanted to improve my knowledge of finance and also experience living overseas. Until that point, I'd never been to the West, not even for a short holiday. I went to the British Council in Singapore to research living and studying in the U.K. I also found out about the Chevening Scholarship, which would potentially fund the cost of me doing a master's course in Britain. The idea of studying overseas on a scholarship excited me.

I didn't apply to any universities in London because I knew I wouldn't be able to afford the living costs there, even if I did get the scholarship. I discovered that Lancaster University, a college in a rural part of northern England, offered an MSc Finance program that was comparatively affordable and had a good ranking. Living there would also be much cheaper than in a big city. I applied and got a place on the program… but… I didn't get the Chevening scholarship, so I decided not to pursue the master's.

Just a week later, however, I began to reconsider my decision. I recalculated whether I had enough savings, which I'd worked hard to accumulate over two years, to cover my tuition fees and living costs without the scholarship. If I dropped my plans to travel around Europe after graduating, I worked out that I could survive for about 10 months of the year-long degree. No one around me, including my family members, was encouraging me to do the course. To them, it simply didn't make sense to give up a good job so soon in my career. Besides draining all of my savings, I'd also miss out on a year's salary. Most of my peers had steady jobs and were feeling comfortable because the Singapore economy was performing well.

But despite the risks to my career and finances, I still went to Lancaster. I thought that if I ran out of money during the final months, I'd just have to use my credit card. I considered the costs involved to be an investment in myself, which would help me land my dream job in structured finance. Being a city boy who hadn't travelled outside of Asia, I also felt that living in the countryside and being in a Western country would be a great change of environment. I'd never seen sheep in my life, but there were plenty of them in the farms that surrounded Lancaster's modern campus!

Did making the "risky" move to Lancaster pay off in the way I'd initially intended? Not immediately. But my MSc boosted my career in the long run. After working in the middle office for four years, I finally managed to get a job in derivatives structuring. I put the skills I'd learned at Lancaster to good use in that role. I also discovered an interest in teaching when I was at Lancaster. One of my professors, Dr TS, was an industry practitioner (he worked for Barclays' original investment banking arm). While I found him a bit arrogant, his teaching had a lasting impact on me, and he also showed me that it's possible to work in banking and teach at the same time.

Living outside of Singapore also made me less naive and more culturally aware, and it gave me an international perspective on life. When I first arrived in the U.K., I was shocked to see Caucasian construction workers because in Singapore in those days white people only did high-level jobs. My MSc cohort was very diverse, and I was able to meet and discuss ideas with people of different backgrounds from all over the world.

Some people think that moving is a big risk — and it can be. But for me, it was riskier to stay behind. If I'd remained in Singapore in the same job function, my career risked stagnating because my skill set would have been too narrow and my experience much less international. My move to the U.K. didn't bring me instant rewards, but it still changed my life.

Shifting to Shanghai

In 2005, I was working for a U.S. bank. Chinese financial services was starting to boom as China liberalized the sector, and I wanted to be part of this growth. I asked for a transfer from the Singapore office to Shanghai. My bank had recently moved into a shiny new building in Shanghai and there were opportunities for me to train junior staff there, so in many ways it was a good time to go. There were also some risks involved. First, I was doing quite well in my job in Singapore and had a good local client network. Moving to Shanghai would require building up relationships from scratch in a new market, while also adjusting to Chinese business culture. There was no guarantee that I'd be successful covering Chinese clients. Second, the Chinese market is huge. Coming from a small country like Singapore, I wasn't so confident that I was capable of leading a team there. I still decided to go for it.

The cold winters in Shanghai and driving on the opposite side of the road from Singapore took some getting used to. But I eventually settled in, and being there was fantastic for my career. No amount of visiting China could have given me the same experiences I had actually living and working there, especially at that critical stage for its evolution as a financial center. On 21 July 2005 at around 6 pm, I received a text from a colleague telling me the renminbi (RMB) would be unpegged from the U.S. dollar. "He must be joking!" I thought to myself. The RMB had been pegged to the greenback at 8.28 since 1994. Reading the official news confirmed China's new currency policy. That was a momentous event to witness firsthand during my time in China.

I certainly took a risk when I relocated to Shanghai, but I really enjoyed my time in China, and I reaped rewards from it over the long term. Many of my Chinese colleagues and clients became friends whom I keep in touch with to this day. The knowledge and networks I gained in Shanghai enabled me to take an even better job in Hong Kong after a couple of years. I also improved my Mandarin skills and was able to teach at top Chinese universities in my spare time. If I'd stayed in Singapore, there was again a danger that my career would flatline.

The Power of Taking Small Risks

The risks you choose to take don't always need to involve big decisions like moving countries. When I worked in investment banking in Hong Kong, my first boss required me to line up three meetings before he'd approve a business trip. But if I had a strong reason to see one important client, I'd just go ahead and make the booking because a delay could mean losing a slot in their busy schedule or even missing out on clinching a deal. Clients rarely wait for bankers. I'd then tell my boss about my travel arrangements and say that if I couldn't set up two more meetings I'd be willing to cover my own costs. I was taking the small risk of my expense request being rejected because I knew how valuable these client meetings were to me. Adopting this kind of mentality paid off. Being prepared to spend my own money to see a key client of the bank would typically persuade my boss to approve my expense claim.

If you haven't reached the stage of your career where business trips are on the cards, you can still take calculated risks. You could ask to work on a project with another department, or start to make more decisions without always asking for your manager's opinion. If you make mistakes along the way, these will help you grow as a professional.

Before making a decision that involves risk, make sure you'll get something out of the experience even if you fail in your primary objective. For example, if I hadn't been successful in covering Chinese clients in Shanghai, at least I would have gained valuable experience of Chinese business culture. Also be prepared to play the long game once you take a risk. I achieved my goal of working in derivatives structuring four years later than expected.

All investments involve risk, including the ones you make in yourself, whether you're an employee or entrepreneur. But if you don't invest in your career, you'll get left behind and end up with outdated skills, especially in an age of rapid technological progress. The risks of remaining where you are often outweigh those of making a change.

40

Make Your Own Blessings in Disguise

My visit to London was going smoothly. It was a personal trip that I'd planned in advance, and I was making the most of my time there by meeting some new connections as well as friends and colleagues from my bank's London office. So far so good! Then I received a message from my firm back in Hong Kong telling me to cut short my holiday because some urgent work had unexpectedly cropped up. I was naturally disappointed, but last-minute changes were part and parcel of my job. I canceled most of my remaining meetings, rebooked my return flight, and headed to London's Heathrow airport.

I also started thinking about how to turn the curtailment of my trip into a blessing in disguise. Before taking my seat on the plane, I decided I'd try to strike up a proper conversation with whomever was sitting beside me, which isn't something I normally do on a flight. After introducing myself to the woman next to me, I mentioned my keen interest in photography. She told me she worked for a company that had a license to make cameras under the brand name of a company once renowned for making film. She was going to Shenzhen, over the border from Hong Kong, to collect the first production sample of a 360-degree camera that could be used underwater. I was fascinated as she told me all about the groundbreaking new device.

Three days after we landed in Hong Kong, I hosted a dinner for her at my favorite Japanese restaurant. She gave me one of the cameras to test out. I was the first person outside her company to use it! I had a fantastic time over the next few days playing with it. I shot a fun video of my kids heading down a waterslide and splashing into a pool. Having to return early to Hong Kong wasn't so bad after all because I had such great experiences after I got back — all the result of my small action of chatting during the flight.

A Profitable Dental Appointment

I've had another blessing in disguise after rescheduling a flight. I flew to Singapore one Friday so I could catch up with family and friends on Saturday before returning to Shanghai the following day. On Saturday night, however, my braces broke and my dentist in Singapore wasn't open until Monday. I decided to stay in Singapore for an extra day to get my teeth sorted out because I didn't fancy taking a long flight with a dental problem.

This still wasn't a great situation. I wanted to be in Shanghai for work, not in Singapore at the dentist. So I looked for ways to turn it into a blessing in disguise, focusing on how I was now in Singapore for all of Sunday and had made no plans. Instead of having a lazy day, I called a real estate agent and asked her to show me a plot of land just south of Somerset MRT station and Orchard Road, Singapore's famous shopping street. A new apartment block would be built there, and as a keen property investor I wanted to take a look at the area.

The location was superb, and I decided it would be a good investment to buy a two-bedroom condo in the building. When I got back to Shanghai the agent faxed me (this was more than 15 years ago) the floor plan. I liked it and bought a unit. I still own the apartment, which has increased in value significantly since then. I'm certainly glad I had to change my flight that weekend!

Making the Most of a Move

I'd been offered a great job that someone from a humble background like me can only dream of: managing director at a bulge bracket investment bank. But I had to relocate back to Hong Kong after less than two years because I couldn't convince my new boss to let me remain living in Singapore. Reluctantly, I uprooted my family, sold my car, and returned to Hong Kong. I was enjoying life in Singapore, wasn't pleased about leaving, and was a little annoyed with my manager. But I was determined to make the most of my transfer.

Being a foreigner in Hong Kong, I told myself to attend as many events as I could in my first year in the city to build up my network of contacts. A friend of mine, Lucia, invited me to a networking evening at the Italian Chamber of Commerce. Going to these kinds of events, where I know nobody, is always uncomfortable for me. I'm an introvert who has learned to be extroverted in small doses. After speaking to strangers for a few hours, I usually go straight home to recover. Nevertheless, I went along that night and enjoyed it. I then kept on saying "yes" to invitations that I'd normally have turned down.

A Singaporean client of mine was also transferring to Hong Kong and he suggested we meet at an event organized by the Singapore Association in Hong Kong. I wouldn't usually go to these gatherings because I already know so many Singaporeans, but I'd promised myself to network as much as possible. I made connections at the event and ended up attending several more sessions at the association. One evening I got chatting about my love of Singapore street food. The chairman suggested I give a talk at the association about what business people can learn from hawkers (street food vendors). I agreed and even brought along my own knife and chopping board to show how a hawker cuts up food. The audience had a good laugh listening and watching me perform. Up until then, I'd only focused on financial topics when giving presentations, so this talk marked the start of a much broader career for me as a speaker.

I had initially pushed back against moving to Hong Kong and had hoped to stay in Singapore. But by being adventurous and taking every opportunity to network, the move became a blessing in disguise. My speech at the Singapore Association opened up a whole new avenue of work for me and led to many more speaking invitations and even TEDx talks.

Life is full of ups and downs. When our plans are upset, we often hope that things will by chance ultimately work out in our favor. But rather than wishing for something good to occur, it's better to take action to make it happen. Turning an unexpectedly bad situation to your advantage requires some effort — as I did when networking in Hong Kong — but it's worth it. Next time your life or career throws you a curveball, think about how you could make it a blessing in disguise.

41

Trade Embarrassment for Opportunities

I teach selling skills at several universities across Asia because knowing how to sell is so critical to career success. Selling becomes even more important as you get more senior in sectors such as management consulting, law and investment banking. Partners and managing directors, not their subordinates, are the ones responsible for winning multimillion-dollar mandates.

I include a role-playing game to make my lessons more engaging. I ask for a volunteer to try to sell the benefits (not the features, see Chapter 27) of noise-cancelling headphones. It always takes some cajoling before someone finally agrees to be the salesperson. Most students feel embarrassed and afraid that their sales pitches will fail. But the person who benefits the most from these classes is the volunteer. Even if they don't perform so well and the experience is a little uncomfortable, they still learn from their mistakes and they remember the lesson much better than the others do.

I can identify with the majority of students who sit at the back of the class, never ask or answer questions, and don't put themselves forward for tasks. I was just like that myself at university. But I now realize that if we can get over our embarrassment, we can open up new opportunities to interact with people.

From Stranger to Mentor

A few students in every class tend to be more proactive than others. I was teaching negotiation skills at Schwarzman College, which is part of Tsinghua University in Beijing and is home to an annual cohort of fully-funded postgraduate scholars from across the world. Jake, an American Schwarzman Scholar, approached me after my lesson to ask if he and a classmate could meet me for a chat during my stay in Beijing. He wanted to learn more from me. I had a busy schedule, but I agreed to meet the two of them at my hotel after a dinner I was having with a client. We chatted in the lobby and Jake picked my brain about thought leadership on social media, a subject he was deeply interested in. I then agreed to come back to Schwarzman College and deliver a lecture on it a few months later. Jake and I kept in touch and I became a mentor of his during his time in China.

It takes courage to ask for a meeting with a more senior person, especially if you don't know them. You could easily get rejected and feel embarrassed as a result. But if you come across someone inspiring, you should go for it because one meeting might be enough to change your thinking, and sometimes your life.

Contacting the CEO

A social media company in China sought my help to invite a chief executive from the banking sector to participate in a "CEO asks CEO" campaign, in which leaders of large companies pose high-level business questions to each other via video. Although I wanted to lend a hand, I was hesitant. I didn't know any bank CEOs well enough to invite them and thought it would be embarrassing to contact one out of the blue. I feared that I'd probably be rejected or ignored by someone so high up. But I was inspired when I thought back to the impressive students who'd reached out to me over the years. They'd taught me not to be embarrassed when asking for help, and that receiving a "no" in reply isn't that bad.

I mustered up some courage and sent a message directly to the China CEO of an American bank. I knew it was important to get the tone of my request right. A hard-sell approach wouldn't work well on a chief executive, so I began by mentioning my knowledge of his bank's plans to take full ownership of its mainland operations. I also suggested he might like to talk about the equity capital market during the video shoot because I knew that was his area of expertise. Most importantly, I didn't ask him outright to participate, but merely enquired whether I could send him a slide deck with details of the project. I made it easy for him to say "yes", but my expectation of receiving a positive response wasn't high.

To my surprise, the corporate communications team from his bank got in touch the next day to ask for the deck. The CEO went on to shoot the video. The campaign was a great success. For me, helping the social media firm secure the CEO interview ultimately outweighed my initial feelings of embarrassment.

Be the First to Ask a Conference Question

When I attend a conference, I sit at the front if possible and ask the opening question during the Q&A. Many of us are too shy to put up our hands and signal for a microphone before anyone else. But if you wait for another person to break the ice, there's typically then a rush of questions and you miss your chance. So try to ask the first question, and make it an insightful one. Why bother doing this if you feel embarrassed standing up in front of hundreds of people at a crowded event? You not only get to hear the speaker's answer, but it also makes it easier to strike up conversations during the networking session that follows — and these networking opportunities could lead to fruitful new relationships. Rather than beginning a chat with small talk, people will say, "that was a very good question you asked at the Q&A. What did you think about the reply?"

A fear of failure is the main reason we feel embarrassed and don't take action. Perhaps we fear our conference question won't be relevant enough, or a senior person won't want to meet us, or that our role-play won't work out. But if you only act when you think you're assured of success, you greatly limit your options in life. Trade embarrassment for opportunities.

42

A Pivot From Hong Kong to New York

I'd just finished lunch with my client at a teppanyaki restaurant within a hotel in Hong Kong. I walked out of the restaurant and there was my tailor, Charan, waiting for me with my newly made suit. I'd messaged him two weeks before my business trip from Singapore to Hong Kong asking him to make me another one of my navy-blue suits, using the same fabric as before. I was a regular customer of Charan, so he already had my measurements.

My schedule in Hong Kong was tight and I could only spare 15 minutes to try on the suit, so Charan had kindly agreed to come to the hotel. We went into the hotel's plush bathroom, which had a full-length mirror. I changed into the suit, and Charan did a final fitting so he could make some minor adjustments to the back of the jacket and the waistline of the pants. I must have put on some weight since I had last seen him.

Charan headed back to his shop in Kowloon and I walked to Central for my next meeting. When I finally returned to my hotel room that evening, I saw that my suit had been delivered and the hotel staff had hung it up in my wardrobe. I inspected the suit again: not only was my name sewn into the inner pocket, Charan had also inscribed it into the coat hanger. That was an unexpected personal touch! The suit was wonderfully well made. The pants even had a hidden pouch within the right pocket, designed to fit my mobile phone and prevent it from moving around or falling out. I was very pleased with Charan's efficiency, workmanship and customer service.

But going the extra mile for his clients wasn't enough of a differentiator for Charan to succeed, at least not in Hong Kong. Tailoring in that city is a competitive industry, so bespoke suit prices are much lower than in London and New York. Charan was only in his late 20s when I first met him, and was up against tailors who were vastly more experienced. As an Indian, Charan didn't speak much Chinese, which made it more difficult to serve Chinese-speaking clients and forced him to focus on the smaller expat market in Hong Kong.

After a while, it became clear to Charan that he wasn't valued enough as a tailor and wasn't making enough money to carry on in the same way. He had to change tactics. Charan started travelling to major cities in the U.K. and U.S. to take orders. He booked hotel meeting rooms in places like London, New York, Chicago and Boston, advertised his services in advance, and lined up appointments for professionals to get their measurements done. The suits were still made in Hong Kong, enabling Charan to charge close to Hong Kong prices in cities where people would typically pay at least three times more for suits of a similar standard. His business eventually took off, so much so that he needed to fly to the U.S. twice a month to take orders.

When Charan's tailoring business initially didn't do well in Hong Kong, he didn't give up. Instead he stayed in the industry he loved, but pivoted to a new market that valued his services. He now had two big differentiators: his pricing was attractive to British and American customers, and he was willing to travel frequently, unlike most of the older Hong Kong tailors. Charan's story teaches us that we must be ready to change our career plans when the competition is too strong.

When I started my speaking career, I tried to compete in the open market for speaking gigs. I quickly became disheartened and felt unvalued. I realized I was just one of many people from multiple industries bidding to speak on topics such as leadership, innovation and sales. Some of them were much more polished presenters than me, while others had a more outlandish stage presence. I wasn't prepared to dye my hair or wear a colorful suit to get myself noticed on the speaking circuit! My fees were being driven down by the competition.

But I didn't abandon my speaking ambitions. I instead changed my strategy and focused on the more niche market for financial events, where my experience as a finance professional helped me stay relevant. While I was competing with speakers who were fairly senior in the finance sector, not many of them had the social media presence I had to attract a large crowd. This refocus was a small action, but it delivered great results because I now no longer need to compete on price to win speaking assignments.

If you feel undervalued in your job, identify where your skills and experience are more needed and try to pivot your career in that direction. For Charan and me, this involved changing the markets we served. For you, it could involve moving teams or even countries.

Charan could have tried to save his business by cutting down on customization and service, but these factors are important to his identity. Pivoting to the U.K. and U.S. markets meant he was still able to keep making high-quality suits. I'm pleased to be one of the few clients who Charan still personally serves in Hong Kong. And he should be glad that I won't be trying to order any cheap colorful suits from him!

Part Eight

Transform Yourself: Develop New Passions, Learn New Skills

43

Unleash the Power of Human Capital

To become successful, you need three types of capital: financial, social and human. Financial capital is the money you have at your disposal. Aside from letting you purchase basic necessities, financial capital can advance your career — for example by attending training courses, buying video equipment to speak at online conferences, or hosting networking events.

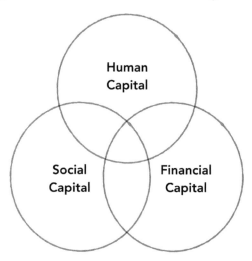

You won't get anyone to come to your networking sessions without having some social capital (which I discuss at length in Part Three). But to build both financial and social capital, you must establish some human capital first. By this I mean your hard skills, knowledge and experience. Let me explain.

Getting Good at Math

I was a pretty terrible high school student. By the time I was 15, I was getting bad grades for quite a few subjects, had poor social skills, wasn't confident, and didn't excel at sport. In short, I had no human capital. With important exams on the horizon, I decided to ignore other subjects and focus solely on mathematics. The amount of effort I put into my math studies is beyond most people's imagination. I memorized the square root of 2 and 3 because these numbers often came up in exams and I could get through the questions faster if I knew them by heart. I did the same past years' exam papers so many times that I already knew some of the answers even before I started working out the solutions. After about a year of intense study, I passed math with flying colors!

My newfound abilities in math finally gave me some human capital. I'd achieved this by relentlessly concentrating on just one discipline (my grades in English, history and literature were still awful), but it made a big difference to my life. Suddenly, my classmates were coming to me for help with math.

> "Hey Eric, can you help? I couldn't work out the answer to question 13 for this past-year paper."
> "Oh, for that question, the answer given at the back of the book is wrong, Samantha. Here's how to calculate it correctly."

As a result of my human capital in math, I established social capital with my peers: they "wanted" me. I started to get invitations to some of their get-togethers, and my self-confidence picked up. One of the best ways to achieve social capital is to help others before you need assistance yourself. But your help must be worthwhile. Although as a teenager I was polite and tried to be helpful, that didn't count for much. It was my math expertise that finally made me useful to other people. This shows that you can't create social capital without having human capital first.

After I became very good at math at school, a few parents started paying me to give private math tuition to their children a year or two younger than me. I was able to build some financial capital because of my math skills. It wasn't a lot of money, but was good enough to buy food at high school and university.

A Transfer of Credibility

During my first year of teaching as an adjunct associate professor of finance, I treated my students as if they were analysts and interns at a bank. I picked on people at random and asked them difficult questions. My tone was often unfriendly. When a student arrived more than five minutes late to a lesson, I'd tell them off in front of the whole class, reminding them that punctuality is critical when meeting clients.

After the year was over, I received bad feedback from students. To them, I'd come across as a harsh banking practitioner. I'd been trying to give them a taste of how tough life can be in the workplace, but my approach had backfired. When I discussed this criticism with the professor in charge of the finance program, he told me that it always takes time for practitioners to adapt their style to teach at university. He said that because I was good enough to have a successful banking career, he was confident I could improve and that my class would run more smoothly the following year.

I had a lot of human capital in banking, so the credibility I'd established in that sector was transferred into teaching. The professor gave me a second chance to prove myself as a teacher. I lived up to his expectations. I'm a better, more empathetic teacher these days, and I create a classroom environment that's best for learning rather than one that mimics the workplace. I now have human capital in teaching and with this comes financial capital (although not a lot) and social capital (executives within my network come to me when they want to hire talented interns or juniors).

In Chapter 1, I discussed the benefits of developing an additional skill set and becoming what I call a "combo specialist". But to add new expertise to your resume, sometimes you first need to be super good in one thing. When you establish your credibility in a particular field — whether it's math or banking or something completely different — you're more likely to be given a bit of slack when you want to venture into a different area.

179

Some of us like to improve several aspects of our careers or lives all at once, but without a "superpower" skill that risks spreading ourselves too thin and not creating the human capital we need. It's often better to choose one skill, spend as much time on it as possible, and become a trusted expert that other people turn to for help. This gives you a solid foundation of human capital upon which you can add new skills, and build both social and financial capital.

44

"Follow Your Passion" Can Be Terrible Advice

"Follow your passion" can be terrible advice because it assumes you actually have a passion, or something you feel a powerful emotion for. The truth is that most of us don't have any genuine passions, and as a result, we feel there's something wrong with us. "Find your passion" is also bad advice because it assumes your passions are lying around somewhere and you can locate them without much effort. But passions usually can't be found; you won't simply stumble across them. They can potentially be developed through trying out a lot of things over your lifetime, but even that's no guarantee of success.

The good news is that while the activities you try may not become passions, they may well become interests or hobbies. You should aim to have a wide range of interests and not worry about whether any of them turn out to be passions.

We also need to be patient as we seek new interests. I didn't wake up one day to miraculously find that I enjoy writing. In fact, I used to hate writing. As an engineer by training I preferred dealing with numbers rather than words. I acquired a fondness for writing only after I'd blogged on social media for several months and received good feedback from my followers.

Why We Need a Variety of Interests

Having interests isn't about financial gain and it's not always about career advancement. I strongly believe that broadening our knowledge makes our lives much richer and more satisfying. With each interest we cultivate, we have the opportunity to talk to new people outside our usual circle. My interests may not be passions, but they enable me to strike up conversations with artists as well as business owners.

My interests make my days more diverse. In the morning, I chat with food sellers about local food heritage. At lunch, I eat a cheap cheese toastie at a university canteen while having a conversation with academics about the future of education and how best to prepare students for their careers. In the evening, my architect friend takes me for an architecture tour of my city.

Recent scientific literature suggests that learning new skills may assist with "neural plasticity", the ability of your brain's neural networks to change through growth and reorganization. The extent to which learning may help "rewire" the brain is a subject for the scientists. But from my anecdotal experience, adding new skills can certainly prevent our lives from stagnating. I've come across many people, from rich successful professionals to those on more modest incomes, who've given up exploring potential new interests and now prefer to focus on accumulating material possessions. I think their lives are poorer and more mundane for it.

How to Find New Interests

I'm a course junkie. Over the past few decades I've enrolled in dozens of courses — from computer programming and video editing, to interior design. I've also recently chalked up a graduate diploma in positive psychology. Although my initial motivation was collecting training certificates, I still find that attending courses is an effective way to develop new interests. But these days you don't have to do a course or read a book to learn. YouTube and LinkedIn Learning videos are excellent resources to help you jump right in and potentially develop new interests. Free webinars are also worth exploring.

Why Passions Don't Matter So Much

I have many interests, but I don't feel an overwhelming passion for any of them. I'm not even passionate about the things I've spent half my life doing. I was interested in banking when I worked in that sector because I enjoyed solving client problems and training young employees. But I didn't like dealing with the office politics. There were too many drawbacks for banking to be a passion. Although teaching greatly interests me, I'm not passionate enough to teach full time. The marking of papers and other administrative work would get me down. Similarly, I wouldn't want blogging to be my main job because it would involve writing under pressure rather than writing for pleasure.

When I hear people say, "do what you love and you'll never have to work again", I have to disagree! It's not easy to find a job that you're passionate about and that still pays a decent wage. And even if you do, the role will usually come with unpleasant elements and you'll soon fall out of love with it. For most of us, it's best not to become too fixated on seeking out passions — it could well be a fruitless search. Developing interests, by contrast, is something we can all do if we put in the effort.

If you then incorporate your interests into your job (see Chapter 6) or make money from them, that's great, but you don't need to. Your interests are of enormous value to you regardless of any monetary benefits. They can make you a more engaging person, expand your social and professional network, and generally help you lead a more enjoyable life. So forget about following or finding your passion; just learn something new every year!

45

Because of Our Differences We Are One

It's well recognized that people from elite backgrounds have innate advantages when they're working in elite professional service firms.

> "The children of the rich and powerful are increasingly well suited to earning wealth and power themselves. That's a problem."
>
> *The Economist* (Briefing: America's Elite), 22 January 2015

> "The U.K.'s most elite financial services and legal firms operate a 'poshness test' that systematically locks talented working-class people out of high-flying jobs, an official report has found."
>
> *Financial Times*, 15 June 2015

I've met many elite students and graduates during my career. They're invariably both smart and socially connected. Their parents' network provides them with access to good opportunities. They learn about taste, etiquette, conversational styles, and presentation skills at a young age, well before they enter university. However, as someone from a humble background, I think non-elite students can still get elite jobs (and succeed in them), if they're prepared to put in extra effort.

Contribute in Your Own Unique Way

I was reading the 2015 book *George Yeo on Bonsai, Banyan and the Tao*, a collection of writing from Singapore's former Minister for Foreign Affairs. One passage jumped out at me:

> "Drafting a speech for the Holy Father, Cardinal Schotte inserted a sentence for the Pope to say that 'despite our differences, we are one'. John Paul II gently chided him and replaced 'despite' with 'because of'."[1]

"Because of our differences, we are one": isn't this statement beautiful and profound? Imagine everyone in an orchestra playing the same instrument. It would sound awful! The same applies at work. Graduates from non-elite backgrounds are different from their elite counterparts and we shouldn't pretend otherwise. But don't worry. Companies are looking for employees who bring different perspectives to the table.

As non-elite graduates, we can contribute to our organizations based on our own unique strengths and in ways that complement our team. Employers want more diversity in their workforces, including diversity of gender, ethnicity, age and sexual orientation. And just as importantly, they also welcome diversity of socioeconomic background. I think there are three core attributes that non-elite graduates bring to elite jobs that help us stand out from our counterparts.

Knowledge

In the early part of my career, I wasn't familiar with the high-end restaurants in which some of my more elite colleagues were wining and dining their clients. But I did know a lot about street food — where to find the best claypot rice or fish head curry — so when overseas clients visited and wanted a genuine local experience, I took them to try authentic Singaporean cuisine. Similarly, if I was chatting with a client who complained of a sports injury, I couldn't recommend a top orthopedic surgeon like some of my workmates could, but I did know a good traditional Chinese medicine practitioner.

---

[1] Yeo, G. (2015). *George Yeo on Bonsai, Banyan and the Tao*. (A. I. Latif, & H. L. Lee, Eds.) Singapore: World Scientific.

As a young professional, I didn't speak English as smoothly as my contemporaries who'd attended Oxbridge or an Ivy League school. But working in my dad's prawn noodle stall had exposed me to different dialects, so I could speak not only Mandarin, but also Cantonese and Hokkien (similar to the Minnan dialect spoken in the southern part of China). This was advantageous for me in banking because some of the successful local entrepreneurs preferred to converse in their own languages rather than in English.

If you also come from a non-elite background, think about how you can use your unique life skills and experiences to your advantage.

Attitude

When I started my first job, in FX sales, the juniors like me took turns to get takeout lunches for the senior traders. For the elite graduates, that might have come as quite a shock. Some of them had never been told to do something as menial as buying lunch for colleagues before. I wasn't exactly enthusiastic, but I didn't show it. I just got on with the job and headed out to the nearby Amoy Street Food Center or Maxwell Food Center, which were (and still are) very crowded because of their great food options. I had to wander from stall to stall because my colleagues always ordered a variety of dishes. Even the two traders who both loved wonton noodles preferred to get them from two different places.

When I was more senior I started traveling regularly for work. At one stage my bank cut expenses and told us to fly economy. I had no problems with that. As a young man, I never dreamed I'd be flying business class and staying in five-star hotels like the Grand Hyatt or Westin. I was even prepared to share a room with my colleague to further save costs. But there were some at my firm who came from wealthy families and had been flying business or first class all of their lives, even for holidays. They were more annoyed by the new policy because the cutbacks represented a huge downgrade for them.

If you're not from a privileged background, you may find that you have a different, more adaptable attitude to life than some of your peers. Make the most of it!

Respect From Clients

If a client only wants to deal with the elite graduates at your company, just refer them to colleagues who can serve them better. In work, as in life, we don't need to capture the entire market. But in my experience, this is a rare occurrence. In fact, some clients respect people who come from humble backgrounds and who've then proved themselves as professionals through sheer hard work. This is especially so with second-generation clients from wealthy families, who grew up rich themselves and tend to mix with other rich people. They often think it's refreshing to talk to someone who's had a less privileged upbringing because they admire your work ethic and value the unique perspectives you bring. They're already familiar with the typical elite career path (Ivy League college, tier-one internship etc.), so they'll find your story much more interesting. Don't be afraid to tell it.

As non-elites, there's no need to feel inferior in the workplace because we can contribute in our own unique way through our knowledge and attitude, and what we bring to clients. But we still need to play by the unwritten social rules in our industries. If we want to succeed in elite jobs, we have to learn new skills and behaviors that we weren't taught at home or university. For starters, it's important to dress appropriately for your job. Your clothes don't need to be expensive; they just need to fit well. If you don't have good social skills, try to develop them. Widen your interests so you can converse socially across a range of topics.

My career proves that this is all possible. As a non-elite graduate, I was at first ignorant about the privileged nature of certain industries. I had no idea that successful professionals often wear expensive watches because I'd never even seen a fancy watch. Once I became less naive about my industry, however, I started feeling inferior about my background. My inferiority complex gradually reduced as my career progressed, and I eventually became proud of where I came from and how it had shaped my attitudes and beliefs.

It's definitely possible for non-elite students to get elite jobs and succeed in them; we just need to put in extra effort at the start of our careers. So stay positive for the long journey ahead.

46

Forget Thinking Out of the Box

We all know that creativity is one of the most sought-after skills across all professional industries. To find new solutions for business problems, you need to get creative. When my students ask me how they can increase their creativity, I never tell them to "think out of the box". That's tired and ineffective advice because most of us don't even know we're in a box in the first place. We're so stuck in a mode of thinking dictated by our job, organization or industry that we don't consciously recognize these restrictions, nor do we see the possibilities out there for creativity.

It's difficult to be more creative — to break and change things — when we're still in the same environment that we've trained in and grown up in as professionals because we've come to accept all the rules and limitations of that environment as completely normal.

You're unlikely to acquire more creativity in your current job. It's better to instead learn new ways of creative thinking from a different place — and bring that back to your work. A good way to do this is by taking a leaf from the arts world. Try out or learn about painting, sculpture, music, dance or another artistic endeavor. Art and design have played an important part in keeping my creative juices flowing, and exposing me to ideas that I wouldn't have come across in the banking world.

Breaking With Tradition

My first exposure to art came when I was an engineering student and I took an additional module on art history. I was the only engineer on the course, but I had a feeling that learning about art would help my creativity. I was taught by TK Sabapathy, Singapore's foremost art historian and critic. He introduced the class to the subject in its broadest sense, from ancient religious art in Asia, to contemporary art in the West. I was fascinated by the art works of each era, and not just in an aesthetic sense.

I learned that the great artists weren't afraid to set new trends, even if they proved controversial. The 19th century Impressionists, for example, broke with convention by painting everyday scenes and using small, visible brush strokes. Their approach initially shocked the art establishment in France. I came to understand that creativity in art involves having the strength of mind to disregard tradition when needed. When I entered the workforce, my knowledge of art history helped give me the confidence to question some of the outdated and inefficient rules that were in place.

The lesson I learned from TK Sabapathy's class stays with me today. When I've lectured at some of the world's top universities, I've taken a rooster bowl — a dish commonly used in Singapore and Hong Kong to serve street food — with me as a prop. If my friends come to my classes, they're surprised that I'd use such a common item during a discussion about banking. But I like to be creative and not follow all the common practices of teaching, so I talk about how bankers can learn work ethics from street food vendors, and I use the bowl to make my point. Art history taught me that creativity is sometimes about breaking away from traditions because that's when you have your best ideas.

The Art of Simplicity

When I worked in Hong Kong, my office overlooked the Bank of China Tower. The building, which was completed in 1990, remains a landmark of the Hong Kong skyline and is famous for its glass-covered triangular frameworks. After looking at the skyscraper day after day, I decided to make a model of it from a big piece of thick gold paper cut into four sections and assembled to match the tower's four triangles. As I was preparing my model, I began to understand the creativity behind the building, which was designed by IM Pei, the Chinese American architect whose other great works include the Louvre Pyramid in Paris. The tower is a masterpiece because it's so simple: it has clean lines and just a few angles.

189

Making the model made me realize that creative solutions, whether in architecture, banking or other fields, don't always need to be complex. In our jobs, we often try to overcomplicate things and we think that the harder the problem, the more complex the answer should be. But simplicity often works better.

Train the Mind With Art

I create my own art and hang it up around the house. One of my pieces contains a dozen tiny key-chain plastic pairs of Adidas Superstar shoes, glued onto an orange piece of cardboard and surrounded by glass. All the replica shoes have their soles face down apart from one, which pokes through a small hole in the glass. I'm trying to illustrate that the first step on any new journey in life is always the most difficult because we have to break through an initial obstacle. The glass panel is not just a protective cover for the miniature shoes, but also a critical part of the art work.

When you produce your own art — or music, or whatever medium you enjoy — you go through a thinking process as your mind tries to come up with new ideas. In doing so, you're training yourself to be more creative. You can then go to work with the same inquisitive mindset and ask questions about the way you work. Getting involved in art has taught me to break with inefficient traditions, find simple solutions, and train my mind to question norms.

I hope that you too can, once in a while, step out of your routine professional environment and use an art form of your choice to become more creative. Perhaps you'll take a pottery or dance class, attend lectures at an art gallery, or try your hand at painting. But if you don't have time for something like that, you have a great creative tool in your pocket: your phone.

Scan the QR code below or go to https://iol.life/smallactions-ch46/ to see the building model and the art work.

47

Learning by Working With Others

I'm a teacher and I also enjoy attending courses myself, but I don't think learning should be restricted to the classroom. Some of my best and deepest learning has happened when I've worked with others. In fact, when people ask me what course they should take on a particular subject, I suggest they should also look at ways to collaborate with someone to acquire the same skills.

Learning Beyond the Classroom

After attending my classes on thought leadership, my students often want to apply what they've just learned. A liberal arts student, Ben, wrote an article about the key takeaways he'd gained from my lecture. He asked me to review it before posting it on social media. I took a quick look and made a few suggestions to make it more interesting. My comments deepened Ben's understanding of thought leadership. By asking for additional and personalized advice after the class had ended, Ben quickly gained a new skill, writing engaging social posts, that were tailored to his needs. He learned by doing: writing a post, incorporating my ideas, and then seeing how his connections engaged with his content. Like Ben, we should all be looking for opportunities for learning beyond the classroom.

Learning Together by Working Together

Natalie, one of my LinkedIn connections, was curious to understand how I was getting good engagement on some of my articles. As a former journalist, she wanted to write an article analyzing my posts to see whether there were any common trends underpinning the most successful ones. I sent her plenty of posts to evaluate. I was keen to take part because working together with Natalie would help me to better understand my readers and my writing. If I'd done the research myself, my own biases might have crept in. I wanted to receive an objective, journalistic assessment of my social media content. Among other useful insights, Natalie discovered that many of my top posts include dialogue. She concluded that these conversations help draw readers into the scenes I describe.

I recently wanted to shoot a short video advising job seekers on creating their own video CV/biography. I didn't have time to study filming and editing skills, so I decided it would be quicker and better to learn on the job. I invited Ray, a film director I know, to make the video with me. No money was exchanged. Ray was happy to participate because he wanted to learn about video CVs. We both appear in the film. I talk about what to include in a video CV and how it differs from a written CV. Ray then discusses the technical aspects of using your phone to shoot the video and using software to edit it. It took us six hours of setting up Ray's equipment and filming to produce a final six-minute clip, but it was all worthwhile. Not only did I learn how to produce a video and tell a story, I also witnessed firsthand how a director plans a shoot, and sets up the lighting and backdrop. More importantly, job seekers found our advice really useful.

Learn a New Skill, Then Offer Something in Return

Sometimes you can learn from a kind soul who's willing to teach you. I wanted to produce video content for "flipped classrooms", which allow my students to learn new knowledge from watching my online lectures at home, so we can then devote classroom time to discussion and problem solving. After watching a series of LinkedIn Learning training videos, I still had a few technical questions to ask about software that helps record your computer screen. I emailed the instructor, Chris, who's based in Los Angeles. He replied and offered to jump onto a Zoom call with me. He gave me some really useful answers and great advice. Because he was so supportive, I invited him to speak during one of my online lectures, introduced him to people in my network, and helped him build his social media presence. We've now collaborated several times, including co-hosting LinkedIn Live sessions.

When people are nice enough to teach you without demanding anything from you in return, don't just accept their help and move on. It's best to bring something to the table yourself, so you can continue the relationship and make it mutually beneficial. My connection with Chris was short term and one-sided at first, but I didn't take his kindness for granted, and we established a lasting relationship that became important to both of us.

Learning new skills from another person in the ways described above is wonderful because it entrenches your knowledge rapidly and efficiently. You learn by doing (often called "experiential learning") rather than by studying theory, and you receive personalized feedback and one-on-one attention. Ben got specific advice to improve his social post, while Chris helped me with my most urgent video questions. Working with someone may also lead you to form a strong rapport with them, enabling you to share skills in the future.

Learning from others isn't as simple as signing up for a course, but the level of knowledge you gain can be much deeper. Seek out opportunities for partnerships, don't be afraid to ask people for help, and be prepared to offer something useful in return.

48

Leverage Tech

"Hey George, I've heard about a job opportunity that may suit you. What's your email address please?"
"Thanks, here you go: george_mikex995@mail.com"
One day later:
"George, your email bounced."
"Oh sorry, Eric, I made a typo in the address. Here's the correct one…"
"Sorry George, I'm afraid the company just found a candidate."

We can miss out on big opportunities by making simple mistakes that cause delays. Knowing this, I'm always looking for tech shortcuts, apps and gadgets that reduce errors and make me more productive. For example, I use keyboard shortcuts on my phone and laptop to generate accurate personal information without having to type things out in full. Each time someone asks for my IOL office address in Hong Kong, I just enter "ioladd" and the whole address appears: "Core E, Cyberport 3, 100 Cyberport Road, Pokfulam, Hong Kong".

I started doing this several years ago because I've long been fascinated by technology and the ways we can deploy it to help improve our lives. I'm also a habitual user of task-management apps. People are always recommending books, films and restaurants to me, but unless I add these to reminder lists on my phone I soon forget the names. I've gained a lot of new knowledge and experiences by doing this, particularly by reading books on my list, although I must admit that some of the movies have been disappointing.

Take Advantage of the Tech at Your Fingertips

Language translation apps are another of my favorite tools. Some people use them to translate the occasional sentence at work or on holiday, but I go much further. After I write an English social media post, I run the whole article through Google Translate, Baidu Translate or DeepL to create a draft Chinese version. These translation platforms have a wide Chinese vocabulary, so they suggest words and phrases that I wouldn't think of. While I still need to tweak the language before I post, the process is much quicker than doing a manual translation. This small action has enabled me, someone who's weak in languages, to publish regular Chinese articles and connect with more Chinese readers.

I also store all my files on the cloud for easy access from my phone. This comes in handy more often than you might expect. During a meeting, a client could ask you an unforeseen question that could open up a new opportunity. Having your cloud drive accessible on your phone lets you provide them with relevant information (e.g. a recent presentation) on the spot. Opportunities come at unexpected times; technology helps you seize them.

I was meeting a client and he said he wanted to learn some financial terms in Chinese. I had a PDF glossary that I thought could help him. It contained more than 300 pages of English names and acronyms — from accelerated depreciation to zero-coupon bonds — alongside the Chinese translations. I told the client, "I'll get it to you right away". I then took out my phone, searched for the file on my cloud drive, and emailed it to him. He was grateful not only for the list, but also for its surprisingly speedy delivery.

Use Tech as a Competitive Advantage

When you use tech to provide someone with a more efficient service, they're likely to see you as a capable person they want to continue dealing with. Tech can also help you stand out if you're an early adopter and deploy it in innovative new ways. I've tried to do this for most of my career. Back in the days before the iPhone, I had a Sony Ericsson candy-bar style phone and I used it as a Bluetooth remote control for my MacBook during presentations.

This was unheard of at the time. When my bank held an offsite in Phuket, Thailand, I surprised my colleagues and clients by controlling my laptop from my phone. They then paid more attention to my presentation as a result.

These days, I always take a phone HDMI adapter to conferences I speak at, so I can connect my iPhone to the presentation screen. This allows me to show people how apps on my phone work in real time, which is a more effective technique than using a static PowerPoint. Not many speakers use their phones on stage, so I'm able to give my audiences a different experience — all because of a simple adapter.

During the early stages of the pandemic, when video conferencing via Zoom and other platforms became the norm, I bought a high-end microphone and camera. Participants commented on the good picture and sound quality of my virtual events. In a competitive market, the technical aspects of my webinars are critical to my success, so I try to stay one step ahead. I've also purchased a live production switcher, which allows me to alternate between cameras at the press of a button in the middle of a presentation.

Technology changes quickly and things that give you an advantage today may become commonplace within a year. This is why you need a "tech mindset": you should be constantly on the lookout for new apps and gadgets that can help you improve your life and your performance at work. You should also find new ways to exploit existing technologies.

Free tech (e.g. keyboard shortcuts) can be great, but you should be prepared to spend money on tech because even cheap gadgets like an HDMI adapter can work wonders. When you're choosing which app to download, don't rule out the $20 option; you may well find that it's better than its free competitors. A small investment in technology can deliver powerful returns, and hopefully ensure that you don't make a typo and miss out on job opportunities.

Part Nine

Life Hacks: Make the Most of Your Money, Health and Time

49

Not a Rolex, but a Timex

Making managing director, partner or another equivalent title is often the highlight of anyone's career. Many people mark the milestone by splurging on high-end designer brands and upgrading their homes. They don't think twice about spending tens of thousands on a watch, buying an exotic sports car, or building a wine cellar in their basement. What explains this extravagance? Some people need immediate self-gratification. Others mainly want their friends, family and colleagues to see and appreciate their new possessions. Their message is: "I've arrived! Look at my watch and look at my car!" The more global and recognizable the brand, the better.

I'm embarrassed to admit that I reacted like this once when I received a big promotion during the middle of my career. Later on, when I was appointed managing director, I had a different mentality. I didn't splash out to celebrate my achievement, nor did I spend wildly during my time as an MD. My watch was a Timex, not a Rolex. Why did I do this, and why would I recommend that you consider keeping your spending under control even if your salary is rocketing up? There are several reasons:

The Thrill Never Lasts

You typically only enjoy luxury goods during the first few weeks of owning them; the novelty soon wears off. So why bother buying the most expensive brands when there are plenty of good alternatives out there? I find my Muji bags are decent enough when I travel. I don't worry if I have to leave them on dirty floors because they can be cleaned easily.

Expensive Items Aren't Always Practical

Some of the fancy items that senior professionals like buying aren't always practical, especially when you're traveling a lot. Many businessmen wear expensive cufflinks with their French-cuff shirts. But I now avoid this combination. I once forgot my cufflinks on a business trip, and when I realized my mistake it was too late to purchase a new pair. I had to race out before my first morning meeting and buy two bags of bread just to get some twist-ties from them to keep my shirt cuffs together. My focus during business trips should be on serving clients, not on my cufflinks or on that expensive watch I just remembered I left in my hotel room.

Less Expensive Can Be More Personal

Cheaper products can be more effective than expensive ones, especially if you personalize them. I don't write with a pricey fountain pen. As a finance professional, I made bulk orders of Pilot pens with my email address on them. Think of ways you can personalize everyday items to make them appear more exclusive and professional without having to spend a fortune. Perhaps you could have your name embossed on a business card holder or notebook. Or you could buy a small piece of good quality fabric and ask a tailor to make you a scarf or pocket square.

Job Security Isn't Great

Job security isn't great these days as advancements in technology disrupt all industries. If you lose your job, it can be difficult to find one that pays what you're accustomed to. An extravagant lifestyle may be unsustainable because it's linked to your ability to stay employed and achieve ever-increasing budget targets. I was happy each time I got promoted, but I didn't assume my job (and higher income) would last forever.

Arbitrage Opportunities

Sometimes it's possible to take the cheaper option, but not lose any enjoyment in the process. When I want to take someone out to a fine dining restaurant, I often go for lunch rather than dinner. I get the same great food and atmosphere at considerably less cost. When I was based in Hong Kong and went on holiday, I chose nearby destinations in North Asia. I knew it would be cheaper and more convenient to visit places in Southeast Asia, like Bali and Penang, once I returned to live in Singapore. Think about some arbitrage opportunities you can take advantage of in your life.

Delayed Gratification

I waited until I'd been working for eight years until I bought my first car. I could have afforded one a year earlier, just after being promoted, but I wanted to make sure I was doing well in my new job. Similarly, I delayed moving out of my parents' home as a young man. I put my freedom on hold, but was able to save tens of thousands of dollars on rent, and use that money for the down payment of my first property. Postponing your consumption by a year can help you save up (see Chapter 50), and give you more freedom in the long term.

When you get a promotion or a big pay increase, it's normal to want to reward yourself and celebrate your hard-earned achievement. However, remember that success and high spending don't always need to go hand in hand.

50

What is FUM?

You may be familiar with AUM (assets under management), the amount of money a financial institution manages on behalf of its clients. But you may not have heard of FUM. No, I don't mean "funds under management". In this case, M stands for money, and U is slang for you. And F? Well, that's a four-letter word that you've probably already guessed correctly.

FUM isn't about retirement, but it does give you the financial independence to make decisions based on maximizing your own happiness. FUM allows you to be bolder and speak up more at work because you're less concerned about the financial consequences of losing your job. This in turn gives you the confidence to take some calculated risks in your career.

I'm fortunate to now be in a position of financial independence. I can choose to do work that pays less, but gives me more satisfaction. Receiving feedback from students who say their lives have changed for the better after attending my lectures or reading my blog posts makes me as happy as clinching a big banking transaction does.

Starting the Long Journey to FUM

In the early part of your career, FUM usually seems like a pipe dream. I reached financial independence only after many years of working hard and spending below my means. That's why I think we should start saving for a more independent future as soon as we have set aside sufficient money for self-development. Even if we never achieve full financial independence — the ability to permanently ditch our day jobs to focus on other interests — many of us can build up enough FUM to last us at least two years without having to work.

I'd recommend saving a small double-digit percentage of your income as FUM, if possible. This may not sound like much at first, but over a few years it can add up to a significant amount, especially if you increase your savings percentage each time your income goes up. Let's say you're currently making $5,000 a month and saving $1,000 of this. Your boss calls you into her office and tells you she'll be giving you a 10% increment. Don't brush this off as an insignificant amount. The $500 salary hike takes your monthly wage to $5,500. If you now decide to channel all your pay rise into your FUM savings, you immediately increase your monthly FUM contribution by 50% to $1,500. This allows you to reach your savings goal much faster.

If you don't expect to get a pay rise soon, you could consider taking on a side job (see Chapter 2). A small side income can have a big impact. Your basic needs like accommodation, food, transport, simple entertainment, and self-development have already been covered by your main salary. As in the pay-rise example above, you should therefore think of your side income not as a percentage of your salary, but as a percentage of the amount you set aside for FUM.

The Power of Compounding Interest

When it comes to debt, I'm ok with taking out mortgages on properties. But I've always shied away from car loans and credit card loans, many of which have very high interest. A monthly credit card rate of 2% works out at 26.8% per year because of compounding interest. This cuts both ways. You shouldn't underestimate the power of compounding interest earned on your long-term FUM savings. It may not seem particularly appealing to put the money you were going to spend on a car into an investment with a 5% annual return, but over 20 years that investment will generate a gain of 165%.

Devote Time to Thinking About Your Investments

Investments that pay fixed interest are just one way of creating some FUM over the long term. I've also become financially independent through making fairly simple investments in stock, real estate, and real estate investment trusts (REITs). I keep it simple because having worked in banking, I know that the returns of an investment aren't necessarily correlated with the complexity of the product.

I've been lucky to have made money from some of my investments as I've rode the twin waves of Asian growth and the tech boom. I don't trade the stock market regularly; I make long-term trading decisions about once a year. This chapter doesn't aim to provide specific investment recommendations because I don't pretend to be an investment expert outside the few areas I'm familiar with. Your investment choices are shaped by many factors — including your wealth, risk appetite, location and age — and these vary greatly from person to person. But whatever your circumstances, you should make sure you're completely familiar with what you're investing in: transparency is key. When salespeople sell you a particular investment idea, is it because the product is suitable for you, or is it because it earns them the highest commission?

While most of this book is devoted to developing our careers, we must also spend time to carefully consider how best to invest our money. In my experience, however, a lot of us focus too much on our day-to-day work, and not enough on what to do with the money we generate from our work. You should see money not in terms of the short-term gratification it can bring, but in terms of its ability to give you at least some degree of financial independence later on in your career. Having some FUM, even if it's not the amount you hoped for, can help you lead a more liberated life and do more of the things that make you happy.

51

How to Spend Money

I'm not particularly extravagant when it comes to buying things. But that doesn't mean I'm solely focused on saving money. Experience has taught me that there are times when our careers can benefit from spending money. The money we spend to save time and to build relationships delivers gains over the long term.

Who Says "Money Can't Buy Time"?

The gym in the IFC Mall in Hong Kong's Central district is one of the more expensive places in the city to exercise in, but its fantastic service made it worthwhile for me to join. I could show up with just my sports shoes. Everything else, from exercise clothes to hair gel, was provided. No more storing my wet and smelly gym gear under my desk after my lunchtime workout. I was also willing to pay a bit more for membership because my office was in the same building as the gym. Not having to walk far saved me time on busy days and meant that bad weather didn't stop me from exercising. Money *can* buy time!

When COVID-19 hit, I had to quickly switch from delivering in-person keynotes to giving online speeches. To ensure I produced high-quality webinars, I went on a shopping spree to buy lighting, audio and video equipment a day before the lockdown kicked in. Delivering webinars was new to me back then, so I wasn't sure which items would actually give my presentations a boost. I erred on the side of buying more gadgets.

I didn't want to miss out on one critical piece of equipment when the shops were closed. When ordering online, I don't mind paying an extra charge to ensure my new piece of tech arrives before I host my next event. My thinking is this: if a little cube light will make my webinar a lot better, and benefit hundreds of attendees, it's worth paying for faster delivery.

Paying the Bill to Show Your Appreciation

We shouldn't always spend our money on ourselves, but spending it on other people, including our colleagues and clients, can help show that we appreciate them. Woody, a junior ex-colleague of mine, wanted some career advice, so he invited me to a nice Chinese restaurant with an Instagram-worthy interior. We had a fantastic lunch and a good chat. When we finished our dessert, I asked for the bill, but Woody said he'd already left his credit card with the cashier. He knew that I'd never let him foot the bill no matter how hard he insisted. Leaving his credit card meant I couldn't fight with him to pay for lunch, and it was a great way to show he appreciated the advice he'd received from me.

I've learned from Woody. When people give up their precious time to offer me advice over lunch, I try to ensure there's no embarrassing dispute over the bill. I hand my credit card to the service staff before my guest arrives. This small action, even at an inexpensive restaurant, can go a long way in creating social capital (goodwill).

Red Packets Show People You Care

In Hong Kong and Singapore, during Chinese New Year (also known as Spring Festival), it's traditional to give red envelopes containing cash to younger relatives and junior colleagues. I also gave these red packets to office cleaners and admin staff at my bank to show my appreciation for their hard work. The cleaners always left my desk spotless. My secretary always put in extra effort to ensure I got my preferred flights. I also give red packets to the waiting staff at my favorite restaurants. Whenever I eat there, they remember my name and look after my guests.

The real value of red packets isn't the amount of money you include; it's the gesture of appreciation. When you treat people well, they do the same for you. They're happy to do the little extra things that can brighten up your day and help you focus on your work.

A Place for Elite Networking

When I first became a senior banker, my bank in Hong Kong offered me membership of an exclusive marina club. I just had to pay the monthly fees, which were tiny compared to the upfront membership cost. Overlooking the sea on the south side of Hong Kong Island, the club's amenities include restaurants, a gym, swimming pool, and rooftop tennis courts. But I turned down the membership. I didn't see the need for these facilities. Moreover, the club isn't close to Central, so it's not a convenient place for entertaining guests.

When I told my colleagues that I'd rejected the club membership, some were very surprised. For them, a club's facilities and fees aren't so important. A prestigious club is a place where they can rub shoulders with very senior individuals — from business owners to people in the C-suite of big companies — and expand their circles in a casual setting. Club membership gives them a career advantage. This also made me realize why some people prefer to live in high-end neighborhoods and send their children to prestigious schools: for the networking opportunities. I believe in building relationships through reciprocity, so this way of thinking doesn't come naturally to me. But even if this isn't your preferred way of spending your money either, it's still worth understanding how some people use their wealth to build elite networks.

Making All Guests Feel Special

When I moved back to Singapore, I decided it was time to join a club. I chose one that isn't as expensive as the marina club in Hong Kong, but its historic location in Singapore's civic district and its old-school British atmosphere make it a unique place to entertain guests. I enjoy treating my friends, foreign guests, students and clients to lunches and dinners. The club overlooks the iconic Padang field, home to sports like cricket, tennis and rugby. When you step inside the colonial-era club, which contains several lounges and bars, you can almost smell the history. I hope to make my guests feel special, particularly when I explain the history of the surrounding buildings, such as the former Supreme Court and City Hall, two neoclassical structures designated as national monuments, which now both house the National Gallery Singapore.

There's another advantage of this club for me: it doesn't accept payments from guests. The bill is charged to members at the end of each month. This means I don't have to worry that people like Woody will leave their credit card behind the bar when the meal is supposed to be my treat.

It's tempting to spend our excess money on consumer goods that we can enjoy for ourselves, but don't underestimate the benefits of using it to save time or make other people feel special. If you prefer not to buy club membership or dinners at fancy restaurants, try entertaining people in other ways, such as buying them coffee, taking them to your favorite street food stalls, or organizing your own networking events. Spending a little money in a thoughtful manner can go a long way.

52

Three Ways to Deal With Stress at Work

Stress is bound to affect you in the workplace, whether you're junior or senior, and it's often triggered by a heavy workload or office politics. Your colleagues may be less capable than you, but they may be good at impressing the boss. I've suffered my fair share of work-related stress, from dealing with toxic people, to meeting tight deadlines and handling transactions that had gone sour.

When I was in banking, one of my clients breached the covenant of a structured financing transaction I'd originated. "I have to get the money back, no matter what!" was the first thing that sprung to mind when I heard the bad news. It took me several weeks to convince my bank to allow me to restructure the deal, while helping the client repay by raising funds from other sources. This was one of the most stressful periods in my working life, and it dragged on for a few months. I even thought about leaving my job, but I felt obligated to recover the loan before I quit. My reputation in the industry was at stake, so I continued working to solve the problem.

How did I get through these worrying months without letting my stress run out of control? There were three main things that helped me, and which could also help you next time you experience a rough patch in your life.

Exercise

An article published by *Harvard Health Publishing* describes how regular aerobic exercise, of almost any kind, has a unique capacity to counter stress, anxiety and depression.[1]

> "The mental benefits of aerobic exercise have a neurochemical basis. Exercise reduces levels of the body's stress hormones, such as adrenaline and cortisol. It also stimulates the production of endorphins, chemicals in the brain that are the body's natural painkillers and mood elevators. Endorphins are responsible for the 'runner's high' and for the feelings of relaxation and optimism that accompany many hard workouts..."

Exercise has certainly helped me deal with stressful situations over the years. The stress relief I get from exercise is quick and effective. I've made a point to incorporate exercise — whether that's hitting the treadmill, lifting weights with a personal trainer, or just going out for a walk — into my tight schedule. I'm not the only busy professional who prioritizes exercise; many successful leaders do too. One manager I know heads to the gym as soon as he checks into his hotel during his business trips. Exercise can put you into a calmer frame of mind for coping with stress.

Diet

There's an expanding body of research exploring potential links between food and mental health. Another article from *Harvard Health Publishing* compares your brain with an expensive car that "functions best when it gets only premium fuel".[2] The author notes that, "what you eat directly affects the structure and function of your brain and, ultimately, your mood".

> "Eating high-quality foods that contain lots of vitamins, minerals, and antioxidants nourishes the brain and protects it from oxidative stress — the 'waste' (free radicals) produced when the body uses oxygen, which

---

[1] Exercising to relax. (2020, July 7). *Harvard Health Publishing*. Retrieved from https://www.health.harvard.edu/staying-healthy/exercising-to-relax

[2] Selhub, E. (2020, March 26). Nutritional psychiatry: Your brain on food. *Harvard Health Publishing*. Retrieved from https://www.health.harvard.edu/blog/nutritional-psychiatry-your-brain-on-food-201511168626

can damage cells. Unfortunately, just like an expensive car, your brain can be damaged if you ingest anything other than premium fuel. If substances from 'low-premium' fuel (such as what you get from processed or refined foods) get to the brain, it has little ability to get rid of them. Diets high in refined sugars, for example, are harmful to the brain."

I think some of the changes I've made to my diet (such as having a more nutritious breakfast and avoiding overeating) may have contributed to improving my overall ability to deal with stress. If you suspect your own diet needs improving, it's worth doing research from reputable sources and seeking professional advice. While I believe in healthy eating and its potential to improve our stress levels, I'm not qualified to make specific food recommendations.

Expressing Emotions

We tend to only show the successful sides of ourselves on social media because we're worried about being seen as weak. But by painting such a positive picture, we make it difficult to share our stresses and anxieties with others, even when we're offline. I'd recommend occasionally publishing a post that reveals your failures or weaknesses (see Chapter 35). It will take the pressure off you to be perfect all the time.

More importantly, it's good to chat about your stress one-to-one with a person you trust, whether that's a partner, friend, or family member. Your stress may linger for longer than necessary if you don't have an outlet to express yourself and you keep your emotions hidden. Friends can acknowledge your stress and offer you support. After talking things out, you may feel that your problems aren't as bad as you thought. The key is to stay in touch with friends and family in good times; don't wait until stress hits you.

Using the three techniques above, I was able to cope with the stress of dealing with work, clients and colleagues. You can't avoid stress in your job, but you can take steps at an early stage to try to ensure that it doesn't overwhelm you. Some problems at work can be solved over time, if you can cope with the stress involved and stay the course. If you take no action against stress, your health may suffer in the long term. If you tackle stress through actions such as regular exercise, eating healthy food, and expressing your feelings, you're more likely to be recognized by your boss, outlast toxic colleagues, and overcome challenges at work.

After 11 long months working to resolve the structured financing deal, I was finally able to recover the full amount and still make some money for my bank. That was a huge relief for me!

53
Why and How to Get Up at 5.30 am

I used to dread waking up early to go to work. Mondays were the worst. As a senior banker, I had to be in the office by 7.45 am to attend weekly morning meetings and give updates about the financial markets and my business.

This all changed when I decided to launch an exciting new project outside of work: my own education and training company. I was naturally waking at 5.30 am (about an hour earlier than before), and I was feeling happy to be up because my life had become more stimulating. I soon discovered that the early morning was a great time to plan innovative strategies for my new venture. I've been rising at about 5.30 am ever since.

The Power of That Extra Hour

I now put my additional hour to good use in a number of ways, according to my needs each day. Here's how having more time in the morning could benefit you.

You Can Focus on Important Long-Term Tasks

We're often so busy that we only deal with urgent tasks involving looming deadlines, like renewing our house insurance, paying a parking fine, or completing our next project at work. But if you want to be successful, you should prioritize tasks that are important but not urgent over those that are urgent but unimportant. Freeing up extra time in the early morning allows you to plan the longer-term and more important parts of your life. You could think about what specific small actions could put your current job back on the right track. Or you could start planning a whole new career journey by reading up on the skills required. You'd be surprised how productive you can be in the morning when you focus on inspiring ideas.

You Can Build Relationships With Senior People

A lot of senior people get up early too. Their calendars won't be so packed, and they won't be dealing with so many calls and emails first thing in the morning. Take advantage of this comparatively quiet period to exchange messages with them, or meet them for a walk and talk (see Chapter 58).

You Can Arrive at Work Early

If you're in a new job or are just starting your career, you should arrive at the office early to get a head start on your work. This helps you create a good impression with colleagues, and lets you focus on the more creative and enjoyable tasks that you might not otherwise have time to complete.

You Can Reflect

Early mornings don't always need to be task orientated. On some mornings, I don't send emails, check social media or read the news. This makes the first hour of my day magical and calm. I go outside to enjoy the silence and smell the refreshing morning air, which puts me in a reflective mood. Instead of planning a specific action, I let my mind wander. I might think about what I'd do if I had a year to live or if I lived to 100. You too can use this tranquil extra hour to dream of seemingly impossible goals that could end up reshaping your life.

How to Get Up an Hour Earlier

Despite the above benefits, many of us (including myself until quite recently) find it hard to wake up an hour earlier than we're accustomed to. Here are three tips to become an early riser.

Make Your Early Morning Tasks Enjoyable

One big reason we don't like getting up (at any hour) is because we usually do so to start jobs that we don't particularly enjoy. So we have little incentive to rise even earlier in the morning. The secret to waking up early is to plan a pleasant task. If you don't believe me, ask avid golfers: they're always willing to play a round, no matter how early they need to jump out of bed. I enjoy reading articles and books when I get up, so I can generate ideas for my LinkedIn posts, speaking gigs, and university lectures. On some mornings, I think about my plans for the week, goals for the decade, or the people I'd like to keep in touch with. On others, I take a mindful walk in my garden to take care of my plants and see things I don't normally pay attention to, like tiny sunbirds feeding on the nectar of flowers. What might you enjoy doing with an extra hour in the morning?

Establish a Morning Routine

While it's good to mix up your morning activities, you should also try to establish at least one regular routine that you always use to help kickstart each day. For example, I drink a glass of warm water just after getting up. Not only do I find this hydrating, refreshing and wakening; it also helps tell my mind that my morning has officially begun. I couldn't do without it. You can also wake up early to exercise, which will help make you feel relaxed and ready for the day.

Go to Bed at a Reasonable Time

I try to avoid late nights. You don't have to be a sleep expert to know that it will be harder to wake at 5.30am if you continually get to bed late.

Waking up early has done wonders for me, and it could help you too. You achieve far more in the serenity of an early morning hour, when your mind feels fresh, than you do after a long and tiring day. Being an early bird can make you more creative: your best ideas might come before some people are even out of bed. Try being an early riser for just two weeks and see how you feel... you may get hooked!

54

Don't Just Manage Time; Manage Energy Too

You're thinking of developing a side hustle or taking a training course, but your ideas have been on the drawing board for months because you lack the time to put them into action. You need at least three cups of coffee to see you through the day and you're too tired after work to do anything other than eat and surf the Internet. I understand how you feel. I've worked many long days during my career.

How have I still managed to pack so many things — banker, lecturer, speaker and writer — into my life? Besides managing time, managing my energy throughout the day has helped a lot. Our days can too easily become dominated by trivial decisions and duties that sap our energy and clutter our minds. That's why I aim to reduce the choices I need to make and the tasks I need to undertake. I try not to waste mental energy dwelling on issues that don't matter so much, which allows me to concentrate on the more important and productive parts of my life.

A lot of us focus exclusively on how we can manage time. But to me, having extra time in our days is usually the desired end result of effective energy management. When you cut back on things that needlessly drain your energy — from useless meetings to mundane assignments at work — you ultimately save time. When your calendar is bursting at the seams and you think you have no time to fit in anything else, step back and assess what you could do to manage both your time and energy better. Let me give you some examples from my own life.

Reduce Trivial Decision Making

If there are trivial decisions you need to make every day, try to eliminate some of them. As you may recall, I always wear white shirts and navy blue suits to work. This conserves my energy. I don't need to think about which color to choose in the morning because all the shirts in my wardrobe are exactly the same. I can select any tie I like because white shirts match all colors (except white!). While this shirt-and-tie example won't work for women, a female friend of mine uses a similar technique. Inside her handbag, she keeps a smaller inner bag that stores stuff like cosmetics, keys and money. Each morning, she simply transfers the inner bag from the previous day's handbag into the new handbag she wants to carry. She saves energy and rarely forgets her keys or lipstick.

Have a Routine

Deciding *when* to do something can take an enormous amount of effort, so have a few things in your calendar that you do at a fixed time. If you have too many time choices (do you go to the gym at 7am, 1pm or 8pm?), you waste energy deciding on a slot, and you may even end up skipping your intended action. Monday 11.30am is gym time for me. Because it's always in my calendar, I know not to book lunch appointments on Mondays. When it gets close to 11.30am, I just pick up my gym bag and go: there's no decision to make.

Plan for the Daily Highs and Lows in Your Energy

My energy levels are higher in the morning, so I prioritize this productive period for completing my strategic work, and I try to keep it free from meetings. Because I'm less energetic after lunch, I like to arrange meetings at 2.30 pm, allowing me to leverage off other people's energy (I don't drink coffee). Your job may not be flexible enough to let you plan your day so precisely. You can't always choose when you have meetings with your manager, for example. But it's still important to be aware of when your energy rises and falls because there may be small changes you can make to your daily schedule, no matter how junior you are. If you're typically tired at midday, try to catch up with your colleagues over lunch instead of in the early morning, when you feel revved up to get work done. Different people have different productive hours. While I'm more productive in the morning, many of my young students experience serious difficulties waking up early. They achieve much more in one hour during the night than in one hour during the morning. Find out when your most productive hour is and do the most important tasks then.

Integrate Your Work and Your Life

Trying to separate our personal and professional lives to achieve work-life balance takes a lot of effort because it's inherently difficult for busy professionals. I manage my life and career together. For example, sometimes it's a more efficient use of my energy to finish critical tasks after office hours rather than wait until the morning when the work is even more pressing. I answer urgent work messages when I'm on leave because delaying my replies would lead to more problems on my return. And if I'm on holiday in a city, I also meet up with my colleagues who live there. Work-life integration cuts both ways. If the people I manage want time off to see their kids perform in the school play, I gladly let them go. When I integrate my life and my work as effectively as possible, my own family benefits from the time savings, while I work hard to give my children an interesting life and good education.

Automate Mundane Tasks at Work

Boring tasks at work suck your energy and time, so try to automate as many of them as you can. When I worked as a risk manager at a bank, I had to obtain end-of-day foreign exchange rates from Reuters and Bloomberg, and email them to front-office traders and back-office colleagues. I soon got sick of doing this, so I wrote a macro in Excel to automate the task. All I had to do was double check the numbers before pressing the "send" button. If you're not an expert in programming, ask a friend or colleague to help you. Automation doesn't always demand high-level computer skills. You're probably on plenty of irrelevant email lists that are hard to unsubscribe from. Instead of manually deleting these emails one by one each day, set up an auto-delete so your email application does it for you.

Extreme Time Management

We tend to think we have 24 hours to play with each day. But when we subtract the time we spend working, studying, sleeping, eating, and doing all those other routine tasks, we likely only have about an hour to ourselves. That's why it's more realistic to think of saving minutes, not hours, from your days. If you can save just 15 minutes a day, that's already about a 25% increase in your personal time. I cut a couple of minutes each morning just by reducing the time I put into dressing myself. I call this "extreme time management". Alongside cuff buttons, men's business shirts typically have a button on each sleeve, but I find these a hassle to fasten, so my tailor makes my shirts with shortened sleeve openings, allowing him to do away with the sleeve buttons. I don't want to waste time and energy tying and untying laces either, so I buy slip-on shoes. My suit trousers have side-tabs, so I don't have to wear a belt, which saves me the hassle of removing my belt and putting it back on when going through security at airports. Is this extreme? Yes. Is it effective? Absolutely!

Note Everything Down

CEOs have personal assistants to remind them of their daily appointments and priorities. Most of us don't. Instead of wasting energy trying not to forget tasks, meetings, ideas, and recommendations, I write down *everything*. A topic I want to research for a webinar, a new restaurant I'd like to try, a revision I need to make for this book, a movie I may enjoy watching: they all go into the notes app on my mobile phone. Whenever I run out of ideas or forget something, I look at my notes.

To help integrate my work and my life, I use the same calendar for everything. I don't want to fix a client meeting when my son is competing in a judo event. If my wife calls me in the midst of a multimillion-dollar transaction to ask me to buy some bread after work, I immediately put her request into the calendar, so I don't need to keep reminding myself to buy the loaf. It's very easy to forget personal tasks when you're busy at work. Buying bread is a small thing, but forgetting to buy it isn't... not when I get home.

Part Ten

A Short, Sweet Guide
to Happiness

55

Lessons in Happiness at Work

We spend more than half of our waking hours working. Our jobs affect our well-being and many of us expect to derive happiness from our work. But there's no mention of happiness in our employment contracts (see Chapter 2). Our employers are already giving us money in exchange for our services and time; they're not obligated to offer us happiness too.

It's up to us as professionals to try to understand how our jobs affect our happiness and vice versa. If you can do this, while not setting unrealistic expectations, you'll be on the path to becoming a happier employee. Here are some of the lessons I've learned about happiness during my career.

Work-Life Rhythm

Work-life balance can improve our happiness, but it's difficult to achieve because technology has caused our jobs to intrude on our personal lives like never before. Keeping our calendars in equilibrium is challenging. We struggle to stop working at the same reasonable hour every day. Working-from-home arrangements blur the line between work and life even more.

It's more realistic to aim for work-life rhythm, a flexible concept that accounts for the peaks and troughs in our schedules. Work-life rhythm is an important part of the work-life integration model that I mentioned in Chapter 54. Instead of trying to finish work at 6.30 pm Monday to Friday, you could do extra hours toward the start of the week, allowing you to leave earlier on Thursdays and Fridays to spend time with friends and family.

You can also attempt work-life rhythm on a longer-term basis. If you're studying for a professional certification while working, you could aim to leave work on time during your exam period, and put in some extra hours once that's over.

Work-life rhythm can be applied to different stages of our lives. In your early career, you may be working in a role requiring long hours, so you can establish yourself in your profession. After a few years, however, you may want to socialize more as you look for a life partner. Once in a settled relationship, work may again become your priority, but if you then have young children, you'll probably focus your attention on your family. And so it goes on.

You Can't be Happy at Work All the Time

Happiness comes from a shift in our mental state, so without this change we can't be happy. If your boss gives you a 50% pay rise today, you'll be jumping for joy! Seeing the higher salary in your bank account for the first time will also make you happy. But after a few months, you'll feel that you deserve the increment and your initial delight will start to fade. After a year, you won't be happy with your pay anymore and will probably be expecting another rise. You should accept the fact that you can't be happy at work all the time, no matter how much you get paid and how well you perform in your job.

Happiness Can't Cancel Unhappiness

You're on a short business trip and the airline bumps you up to first class because the flight is overbooked. You've never flown in first class before, so you're like a kid in a candy store. During the journey, one of the cabin crew accidentally spills coffee over you and ruins your new white top. You're only away for one night and you don't have a suitable replacement, so now you're annoyed and unhappy. Your previous good mood doesn't override your new state of grumpiness. This explains why rich and successful people can be miserable sometimes: happiness can't cancel out unhappiness.

We Need Different Types of Happiness

Like we need many types of vitamins from our food, we also require different types of happiness from our jobs. Here are some examples:

Financial

We all need the happiness that comes with our salaries, whether that's to put food on the table or treat ourselves to something that gives us pleasure like a nice holiday or new phone.

Relationships

We get a lot of happiness from having strong relationships, including work-related ones. Some of us only build relationships with people we deal with directly. But you should try to have a few friends within your company whose roles don't overlap with yours. These relationships can be less competitive and more supportive than those with someone in your immediate team because you're not going for the same promotion or trying to impress the same boss. It's therefore much easier to have open discussions, in which you share your true feelings about work, especially when you're experiencing tough times. The other person can act as a sounding board as you chat to them during a coffee or lunch break.

Interests

If your work is your passion, congratulations, but for most people (including me) it's not. But you can still increase your happiness by incorporating your interests into your work (see Chapter 6) and/or by having a second career.

Meaning

Sometimes your job is intrinsically meaningful. Perhaps you're working for a non-profit organization or in a corporate social responsibility role helping the most disadvantaged people in society. But most of us don't get to make a social impact on this scale. You can, however, still find meaning from work. My father sold prawn noodles from the 1950s until the 1990s. It was a tough job, and he rested only one day a year, but he took tremendous pride in his work. He had what the Japanese would call a *shokunin* (loosely translated as craftsman) spirit within him. He was very particular about the freshness of his ingredients and the standard of his cooking. My father wanted to serve good food. Seeing people enjoying his noodles and coming back week after week made him smile. I once overheard a customer telling him that she had regularly eaten his prawn noodles as a child before she moved overseas. She said she always visited his stall whenever she returned to Singapore because she missed his food so much. Giving customers like her the simple joy of eating a nice meal provided great meaning to my father.

Health

Many of us don't prioritize exercise and health. We focus on our work, family and friends, and neglect to fit exercise into our routine. This is counterproductive in the long term. If we fall into poor health, all other forms of happiness pale in comparison with the misery we face. Having a high income or a meaningful job won't help us. This is why I eat a healthy breakfast on most days and schedule lunchtime workouts at a gym near my office. During periods when I work mainly from home, I take a twice-weekly break to climb 16 flights of stairs in my building five times. Regular exercise can improve our mental health too.

May I wish you an abundance of MMHH: money, meaning, health... and happiness.

56

The Best $2 I Ever Spent

During the middle part of my career I had a performance assessment with my boss. He was happy with my work because I'd done several transactions, but he said I should have given some credit for those deals to my colleagues. I was working in a competitive environment at that time, so I was constantly pushing for recognition of my successes, wary that someone more vocal than me would steal the glory after my hard work. But I took my manager's criticism to heart and reflected on how I'd acted. I didn't feel good about myself.

From that point on I adopted a more collaborative attitude to work. Whenever I executed a large transaction, I sent an email thanking the people involved and allocating credit to them. I made sure I copied in their bosses, so they knew about the good work their juniors had put in. Then I'd organize a tea break and order some donuts or egg tarts (the former were twice as popular as the latter), so we could all come together to celebrate our achievement. If it was a particularly important deal, I'd take the team out for a nice lunch.

When I used to hog the acclaim at work, people still congratulated me for my deals. But they did so in a superficial way; inside they were likely feeling excluded and jealous. When I started sharing credit, my own happiness increased because the atmosphere at work improved and people started treating me as an ally rather than a rival. My boss could see I was a genuine team player and wasn't just strong on the transactional side.

It's natural to want to do all you can to maximize your own visibility in your company, especially if you work for a large organization and feel like a small cog in the wheel. But that's short-term thinking. Over the long term, your career is better served by acknowledging the valuable contributions of your teammates and thereby building lasting relationships with them that will benefit you in the years to come. Your colleagues will be happy to help you succeed in the future because they know they'll be recognized for the part they play in your projects. They'll also be more likely to share new opportunities with you when these arise.

A Random Gift of Kindness

We can derive happiness from giving to other people, just as we can from sharing credit with them. Every Monday lunchtime I have a personal training session at my gym in Raffles Place in downtown Singapore. Afterward, I usually stroll to a nearby food stall that specializes in one of the country's most iconic dishes, chicken rice. I eat this dish every week. One day I was queuing behind a tall young man dressed in office attire.

"A pack of chicken rice please," said the man as he placed his takeaway order.

"That will be $5," said the stall owner.

"Oh, $5..." said the young man after opening his wallet and realizing that he had only $3 (the little chicken rice place didn't accept cards). An embarrassing moment of silence ensued.

"I'll cover for him," I told the stall owner as I handed him $2. The young man turned his head to look at me as if I'd just saved his life.

"Do you have PayNow? I'll transfer the money to you," he said, referring to the Singapore mobile payments platform.

"No, I don't. No worries. Enjoy your lunch," I replied (I'd just moved back to Singapore and I didn't know what PayNow was).

"Thank you!" he said, and he walked away with his chicken rice before disappearing into the crowd in Singapore's financial district.

My small, random gift of kindness made me happy throughout the day. It was the best $2 I'd ever spent. I derived much more joy from it than from eating a $2 chocolate bar. It made me realize that increasing our level of happiness doesn't always demand a lot of money or effort. Whether we're giving $2 to a stranger to help them buy lunch, or sharing credit with our co-workers, we gain so much in terms of our happiness when we're generous and turn our focus to other people.

57

Mr Wizard's Unconventional Thinking

I took the boat to Sharp Island, which lies just off the east coast of Hong Kong and has panoramic hiking trails, clear waters and two beautiful beaches, making it a great place for a day trip. After exploring the main island I decided to walk over the tombolo, a naturally formed sand and pebble bridge that connects Sharp to nearby Kiu Tau islet at low tide. This turned out to be a mistake. As I was making the crossing, the strap on my left sandal broke and I had to spend the rest of the day trying not to trip over.

I was also disappointed about ruining my favorite sandals. They were comfortable ones that had served me well for eight years. When I visited Singapore a few weeks later, I returned to the store where I'd bought them, in the slim hope that they'd still be in stock. The shop is run by a guy whom I addressed as Mr Wizard, after the name of his shop. When I showed him the sandals, he said he had the same pair in the right size. I was surprised and overjoyed!

Mr Wizard is quite a character. He lived in London for 30 years, returned to Singapore, and spotted a gap in the market for specialist European leather goods. He must be in his 60s or 70s now and has bright white hair, but he loves wearing skinny jeans, tank tops and sharply pointed shoes. When I saw him that day, he was sporting silver slip-ons and a black belt. I asked him why he wasn't following the fashion convention, espoused by magazines like *GQ*, of matching his belt and shoe color. He replied, "Life is too short to worry about matching colors, young man! Wear what you like."

This was an epiphany for me. I reflected that we impose restrictions on ourselves based not on enforceable rules and regulations, but on what others (our friends, family, classmates, colleagues and bosses) expect of us. We study hard, land a good job, get married, and then perhaps hit a mid-life crisis and wait for retirement. Our lives can become monotonous and unhappy if we let ourselves become too controlled by conventions.

Looking back, my own career was largely shaped by the times I rebelled against conventions rather than followed them. When deciding which undergraduate degree to pursue, I took the path taken by many of my seniors at high school: I majored in a STEM (science, technology, engineering and mathematics) subject, in my case mechanical engineering. When I graduated, however, I applied for roles in banking, an unusual choice among my engineering classmates. I didn't think banking was necessarily a better job, I just wanted to widen my horizons through exposure to a different industry. My choice broke the career customs of that time. My first boss in banking said I was one of only a few engineers she'd ever recruited.

Breaking with Banking Traditions

Many years later, I was hired by an investment bank in Hong Kong to cover corporate clients. When I came on board, I realized that nobody in the team was looking after financial institutions for my products, so I expanded my original job description and started covering that segment too. My colleagues didn't try to thwart my plans. Within a year, I closed a transaction with a financial institution, and everyone (including me) was happy. I continued to cover the sector. My decision not to impose limitations on myself paid off.

Halfway through my banking career I started teaching at several universities. This was another career move that broke the mold: not many people take a side job while working full-time in an industry as demanding as financial services. It allowed me to live two lives. In universities, lessons are usually scheduled well in advance to secure classrooms and slots in lecturers' calendars. I often knew the exact time and location of my classes six months beforehand. By contrast, in banking, I couldn't be certain where I might be the following week. I might need to hop on a plane at a day's notice should a client suddenly want to see me. I had to hope that my banking work didn't get in the way of my teaching at the last minute. But although balancing my unconventional banking/teaching life was challenging, I also gained valuable new experiences. I enjoyed sharing my practical skills with students and helping HR at my bank hire interns. Overall, I felt happier to be able to add value to them.

A Bilingual Calling Card

These days, I spend time writing on LinkedIn as well as teaching. I write in both English and Chinese within the same post. Most LinkedIn writers stick to one language (even if they're bilingual themselves), likely because they fear that a combined post risks putting off both sets of readers. But I've been taking my unconventional approach for several years now and it's become my calling card. It brings my English and Chinese-speaking followers together to exchange ideas.

Questioning Your Own Conventions

We must, of course, abide by the law of the land and adhere to sensible common standards in our industries and companies, such as dressing appropriately for work. But beyond these commonsense rules, we impose informal traditions on ourselves that don't benefit us and could be abandoned without harming anyone else. It's traditional, for example, for software developers to study computer science. But I've recently met good programmers who've ditched that convention. They've taken degrees in subjects like philosophy to improve their critical-thinking skills, while learning how to code on their own.

Think about your own career and try to figure out whether there are aspects of it that are driven too much by traditions and expectations rather than what's best for you. Can you take an alternative path that could lead to more success and greater happiness? It's a liberating feeling when you realize you're in control and have the power to break the conventions that you've inflicted on yourself for years. It opens up opportunities for widening your perspective and making your life more interesting. Without becoming a teacher and writer, my career would have been limited to the narrow world of banking.

Like most people, I can easily fall into the trap of blindly following conventions when I don't need to. But once in a while I take a step back and think about the words of Mr Wizard. Our belt and shoe colors don't always need to match!

58

Walk and Talk

Life is about achieving your dreams.
Life is about taking actions.
But sometimes life is also about living in the moment and smelling the flowers.
As it snowed this morning, I took a walk along the busy streets of New York City.
The cleaners were already clearing the snow.
Women in waterproof boots were crossing the traffic lights steadily as they made their way to work.
I sat down in a cafe, watching the passersby.

I wrote the above as a poetic LinkedIn post during a trip to New York in early April. Coming from tropical Singapore, snow is always a novelty to me, and I was particularly surprised to experience it at that time of year. It was strange to walk past daffodils, a flower that blooms in spring, and see their yellow petals covered in white. Manhattan in the snow is cold but beautiful, so that's why I made time to walk around, sit in a cafe, and simply take in the world around me. When I left the cafe and finished my walk, I felt happy and relaxed, but also inspired and full of new ideas.

If you're reading this book, you're most likely focused on achieving career success. But we're often so caught up in our busy lives that we don't properly reflect on what success should actually look like. What objectives should we have? What projects could we start? What kind of work makes us happy?

I believe we sometimes need to let the mind wander freely about the possibilities in life because that's how we get our most imaginative ideas. Don't attempt this when you might be easily distracted by your day-to-day activities. Instead, give yourself permission to occasionally live in the moment, even if just for 15-minute stints that you can easily fit into your packed calendar each week. I free my mind by going for walks and immersing myself in nature. If I'm in a park, I look at the different plants and listen to the birds chirping. If I'm in a city center, I find spots of greenery to admire or just look up at the sky. If I'm pushed for time, I take a meander in my own garden and smell the flowers.

I'd recommend giving this a go. For one, walking and reflecting will likely relax you and improve your happiness. Second, as you unwind and become less preoccupied with the immediate pressures of your job, you free up your mind to think about more innovative and longer-term topics. Perhaps you could start planning how to write a LinkedIn post that could open up some interesting opportunities, or decide to send a cold email to an inspiring person who could give you valuable advice.

Going for a walk and being in the moment (a small action in itself) is also an effective way to reflect on what you've read in this book so far and decide how to put these learnings into practice. If you pressure yourself to come up with an immediate "small actions" plan, your thoughts may not flow as clearly. I'm not advising you to be lazy (and that's probably not in your nature anyway), but you'll be amazed by what comes into your mind when you step away from your desk and head outside.

Head Outdoors for Deeper Conversations

Going for a walk alone helps us unleash our own creativity, but walking with another person is a great way to expose ourselves to other opinions. When I want to get advice from someone I admire, I often invite them to a "walk and talk" instead of a meal. Not everyone accepts, but many do (including senior people) because I offer to meet them at a convenient time and location, and I plan a quiet and scenic route that takes about 1 to 1.5 hours to complete.

Why bother with a walk when meeting in a restaurant is the more common practice? For starters, you get some light exercise, you can enjoy the surroundings, and it costs you nothing. More importantly, the discussions you have when walking tend to be deeper. There are advantages of meeting over a meal, especially if you want to treat a foreign visitor or network in a larger group. But when meeting someone one-on-one to receive advice, you face constant interruptions at a restaurant — from ordering, to eating and asking for the bill. When the only other thing you're doing is walking, you can focus almost entirely on the conversation. Your exchange of ideas flows more naturally because there are fewer distractions. Next time you want advice from someone who's more senior (or who has a different skill set), ask if they'd like to walk and talk with you.

Some of the students and young professionals I know don't like walking because they think it's an unproductive use of time. They want to focus on concrete action rather than reflection. But I advise them that these two things are interlinked. We think more creatively (and better absorb innovative thoughts from others) when we escape the confines of our normal indoor environment. And this allows us to formulate better plans to put into action.

If you'll excuse me now, I see from my window that the lotus flower in my garden has just opened. It's the first time it's bloomed this year, so I'm going to take a closer look and have a quick walk outside. I hope to return with some fresh ideas for Chapter 59.

59

Learning From Nature

Many of the plants we see around us have been alive for decades. They've been through bad weather, they've wilted, but they've also survived and flourished. I've always enjoyed being in nature and over the past few years I've taken up gardening as a hobby. I feel especially happy when I'm able to help a struggling plant thrive, or when I see a tree bear fruit for the first time. Gardening has also taught me some important career lessons, which I think apply to most of us, whether we have a garden or not.

Be Flexible, Like My Sandpaper Vine

In my garden I have two pots of sandpaper vine, a climbing plant with dark green leaves and flowers that are a stunning purple color when they bloom. On very windy days, the pot on the right always falls over while the one on the left remains in its place. This puzzled me because both plants are next to each other, are the same height (around two meters), and sit in pots of the same size. To encourage them to grow upwards, the vine in the right pot is tightly secured by wire to solid wooden poles, while the left one is loosely tied with string to two thin bamboo canes. Although the right one appears sturdier, I eventually realized that it catches the breeze easily, while the branches of the left vine sway with the wind. Each bamboo stick in the left pot is supple enough to allow some movement without toppling the whole plant. Although it's not as neat looking as its rigid neighbor, the flexible sandpaper vine is just as beautiful when it blooms.

In our careers, we face many strong winds — including company downsizing, automation, and the COVID-19 pandemic — that can knock us off our intended path. Like my left sandpaper vine, we need to be flexible during these stormy periods. Being flexible doesn't mean being weak; it means adapting to new environments rather than being ruined by them. When the Asian financial crisis hit in 1997, my plan to work in derivatives structuring went out the window, so I changed course and took a role in risk management. After four years I was able to use my experience in risk to get a derivatives job. If you're flexible and willing to make compromises, you can ride out a storm and your career can bloom again.

Expand Your Horizons

The desert rose in my garden has exotic blood-red flowers and a fat trunk that it uses to store water for times of drought. It's nicely shaped, a bit like a bonsai tree. It did exceptionally well when I first bought it, but after about a year I noticed that it wasn't flowering as frequently. I added fertilizer and moved it to a sunnier spot, but that didn't help. When I posted a photo of my desert rose online seeking some advice, someone commented that the roots had outgrown the pot. So I moved it into a larger pot, and soon it started to bloom more often.

Like my desert rose, you may sometimes find that your career isn't blossoming because you're stuck in a role and working environment that are too restrictive to fulfil your ambitions. In this situation, try to secure a lateral move to expand your career horizons. Look beyond your team and gain fresh perspectives by expanding your network with people in other divisions, companies and even industries. And if you work for an international firm, consider applying for an overseas posting, even if it means taking a pay cut or putting yourself in an unfamiliar environment.

The Long-Term Power of Small Growth

When I moved back to Singapore, the street outside my home looked a bit bare. It was public land, so I called the National Parks Board and asked for permission to plant trees at my own expense. I envisaged a row of bucida trees, which have dense overhanging foliage creating lovely natural shade.

The board turned down my request, but sent a representative to meet me just two days later. He explained that we need to be careful about the trees we plant because some have powerful roots that help them to thrive, but can damage drainage systems as they expand over the years. However, he agreed that my street needed more greenery, and after just a few months some workers arrived to plant trees along both sides of the road.

I was impressed by his quick response and I also reflected on what he'd said about the tree roots. A tiny amount of growth every day can have a powerful effect over time. In the case of tree roots in urban areas, the impact can be damaging to infrastructure. But in our careers, regular tiny growth over a long period of time can yield positive results. You could, for example, get to know one new person in your industry every week, or spend slightly below your means with each purchase you make, allowing you to invest in your career. The results may be slow to show, but the impact will eventually be tremendous. I've improved my Mandarin bit by bit over the years. I've watched Chinese movies, used Chinese social media, spoken Mandarin regularly with my Chinese friends, and now I can finally deliver a keynote speech in Mandarin.

When It's Just Not Your Season

I have a huge bougainvillea in my garden. It's a tough plant and flowers almost all the time. By contrast, my orange jasmine isn't always in bloom, but when it is, its scent is so sweet that you can smell it from afar. No wonder its Chinese name means "seven-mile fragrance". Many plants have their flowering seasons, and there's nothing we can do to make them bloom when it's not their time yet.

Some people seem to be successful all year round, similar to the bougainvillea. But most of us experience flat periods between our triumphs, like the seasonal orange jasmine. The latter flower teaches us that we can reach career plateaus and still be happy. If we patiently wait for the season to turn, success will come again.

Add Value to Attract Happiness

A German study on bird biodiversity published in the journal *Ecological Economics* found that being around 14 additional bird species can give you as much satisfaction as earning an extra $150 a month.[1] I'm not surprised by these results. It always makes me happy to see birds and hear their songs, so I buy fertilizer. What has fertilizer got to do with birds, you may wonder? By fertilizing and taking good care of my plants, they will bear the fruits and flowers that help entice birds into my garden. I can't just sit back and hope the birds will come.

Similarly, if we want to make our lives happier and more prosperous, we should try to attract inspiring, knowledgeable and supportive people into our lives. To build good relationships with them, we should always think about what we can do for them. Relationships need nurturing too. This could involve anything from buying people lunch to using our expertise to help them complete a project. When you add value to others first, you build better relationships.

Plants need sunlight, fertilizer and water to keep them healthy — and we require similar things in our careers too. Our sunlight is new knowledge that gives us energy and opens up opportunities. When we spend time with people who inspire and encourage us, they act as a fertilizer to help our careers grow more quickly. And when we take small actions to improve ourselves every day, it's like watering a plant regularly: little by little we start to bloom.

[1] Methorst, J., Rehdanz, K., Mueller, T., Hansjürgens, B., Bonn, A., & Böhning-Gaese, K. (2021). The importance of species diversity for human well-being in Europe. *Ecological Economics, 181*(2021). Retrieved from https://doi.org/10.1016/j.ecolecon.2020.106917

60

A Gratefulness List for Your Job

Spending three hours at the hospital on 31 December wasn't the best way to end the year. A tree branch had hit my right eye while I was outside pruning my plants. My vision had become impaired and there were halo effects when I looked at lights. When I eventually left the hospital late on New Year's Eve, I wondered whether to blame myself for not being careful while gardening, or try to be grateful even though the accident had ruined my plans for that evening. I actually ended up doing both. After blaming myself, I thought:

> I'm grateful to have access to high quality medical care. A senior eye specialist attended to me within hours even though it was New Year's Eve.
> I'm grateful he diagnosed only a minor abrasion to my cornea, the outer layer of the eyeball, and not anything more serious that could have permanently damaged my eye.
> I'm grateful I can still see well enough to write my next book chapter.

It's human nature to focus on the bad sides of life, but we can also choose to be grateful for what we have. Gratitude is important because of its association with happiness, as an article posted by *Harvard Health Publishing* explains:

> "In positive psychology research, gratitude is strongly and consistently associated with greater happiness. Gratitude helps people feel more

positive emotions, relish good experiences, improve their health, deal with adversity, and build strong relationships."[1]

We have many things to complain about at work. There are bosses who unfairly overlook us for promotions, and complex company hierarchies that make it hard to get ahead. But when you have a decent job, even if it's not your ideal one, there's still much to be grateful for. When I was working for a bank in Hong Kong, I went through a period of feeling stressed and unhappy. Then one day I decided to write a list of what I liked about my job:

I'm grateful for the healthcare insurance provided by my bank to my family and me.

I'm grateful for the opportunity to contribute to my company.

I'm grateful for the learning and training opportunities I receive at my firm.

I'm grateful to have flexible working hours and annual leave, so I can spend quality time with my family.

I'm grateful for the intellectual engagement I have with my colleagues.

I'm grateful my office is in a convenient location.

I'm grateful my job involves traveling to different cities, giving me the chance to experience other cultures.

I'm grateful my employer gave me permission to have a side gig, so I can pursue my interest in teaching.

I'm grateful my clients appreciate my service and product knowledge.

I'm grateful to have a stable income to put food and mobile phones on the table.

Writing and thinking about this list gave me a sense of balance. The downsides of my job didn't magically disappear, but instead of dwelling on them, I now appreciated the many good aspects I had previously taken for granted. Most of the things I was grateful for (including my stable income, family time, and medical cover) were in the grand scheme of things much more important than the frustrations I faced in my role. I also realized that

---

[1] Giving thanks can make you happier. (2021, August 14). *Harvard Health Publishing.* Retrieved from https://www.health.harvard.edu/healthbeat/giving-thanks-can-make-you-happier

my problems would have been far greater had I been out of work. I was fortunate that I had a job and that the fundamentals of my role were ok. I started to feel happier.

Now that you've almost reached the end of this chapter, take a few minutes to write a list of what you appreciate about your job. Try to come up with at least 10 points, as I did in the example above. A lot of us overlook simple facts like getting paid each month and gaining valuable experience every day.

This process, which you can do once a month, should help put unpleasant situations into perspective, and put you in a happier state of mind to deal with your challenges. It's natural to feel stress and worry about your job. You spend many hours at work and you probably don't get on with all your colleagues. Just remember to balance your negative thinking with a healthy dose of gratefulness once in a while.

Part Eleven

How to Demonstrate Thought Leadership

61

Letter to the Chairman

I was teaching leadership skills for an EMBA program at one of Asia's top universities. After my lecture, I started chatting with a group of course participants, including Oyama, a senior manager from a Japanese shipping company. I asked him about his interests, and he said he's passionate about sailing.

When he was a junior employee at his firm in Tokyo, Oyama wanted to travel overseas to race his sailing boat. His boss wasn't supportive, so he decided to write a letter to the chairman of the company. I enjoyed hearing the rest of Oyama's story and advised him to share it with his team at work. He hesitated. Oyama wasn't particularly proud of his actions as a young man because he'd embarrassed his boss by contacting the chairman directly. I gave him a few tips on how to structure his story as a presentation. Although still feeling uncomfortable, he agreed to tell his story during an upcoming staff training session. Here's what he said to his team on the day he gave his slide presentation:

Oyama's Story in His Own Words

There are three things you should NOT do at your workplace:

1. Prioritize your personal interests over work.
2. Embarrass your boss.
3. Annoy your co-workers.

(Continued)

247

(Continued)

If you do these, your sail will lose wind, your boat will lose control...
and it will capsize!

But I did all three of them... perfectly. Let me tell you my story:

I was 25. I was reckless. I didn't care about my performance at work.

Why? Sailing was my top priority, and I was training hard at it.

I wanted to go to Lake Garda in Italy with my "49er" boat to participate in the world championships.

It would cost a lot of money and I needed to take two weeks' leave.

To overcome these obstacles, I wanted the company to sponsor me.

In return, I would advertise the company's logo on my boat's
spinnaker — the big sail at the front.

Unfortunately, my boss didn't show any interest in my idea.

I then pitched it to the PR division, but the general manager there
politely rejected me.

Fair enough. Why should the company sponsor a super junior
employee's personal challenge?

However, I wasn't satisfied. I wanted to make my idea come true.

It occurred to me to write a letter to the chairman of the company to
convey the purpose and passion behind my sponsorship idea.

I wrote the letter, waited a few days, but nothing happened.

I started to regret my rash action.

Suddenly my phone rang — the chairman was on the line!

"I read your letter and liked the challenge you've set yourself. I look
forward to having your report from Italy," he said.

When I put down the phone, my hands were shaking.

I spoke to my manager about the call immediately.

He seemed so embarrassed and told me to contact PR again.

I eventually secured the sponsorship. My dream came true.

I had prioritized my passion over my job, embarrassed my boss, and
annoyed my co-workers by leaving them with more work while I was
off sailing. But although I'd broken these rules of the workplace, I'd
learned a more profound lesson in how to achieve goals:

1. Set your purpose
2. Believe in yourself

(Continued)

> 3. Take actions
> 4. Consider options
> 5. Don't give up
>
> To sum up my story: don't let your life be overwhelmed by social norms!

Four Traits of a Great Leader

Oyama's effort in making the short presentation paid off. He confronted a chapter in his career that he'd felt embarrassed about for many years, and turned it into a lesson for younger colleagues. He received positive feedback from his team members, one of whom wrote:

> "Oyama-san, thank you for sharing your private story today. I must say that you are bold and courageous in pursuing your ambition. I really like your last slide. Truly we are our captain of our own life: set the course and reach the destination".

Before the presentation, Oyama was viewed as a capable manager, but afterward his team also saw him as a strong leader who was unafraid to show courage and confidence when pursuing his ambitions. Here was someone whose vision for the department they would be willing to follow. Although Oyama's story inspired me when he told it to me, I particularly admired him for sharing it more broadly with his team members. I think his act of sharing highlights four of the traits that help to make a great leader:

- **Courage**: Oyama was ashamed of the way he bypassed his boss, so he swept the sailing-sponsorship story under the carpet for years. It took courage to finally face up to what he'd long thought of as an embarrassment.
- **Humility**: Oyama is a successful senior manager at his company, but he was still humble enough to accept my advice and to learn new presentation skills from me. He was used to presenting financial data, but this was the first time he'd spoken publicly about his personal life.

- **Willingness to teach**: Oyama is always thinking about how to groom younger colleagues. Although he felt uncomfortable sharing his story, he still went ahead for the benefit of training them.
- **Authenticity**: Oyama didn't disguise his story as an end-to-end triumph. He revealed a vulnerable side by admitting that he regretted sending the letter and by describing his trembling hands after the phone call. Being authentic made it easier for his colleagues to relate to him.

As leaders, it's natural to talk about our conventional successes such as the deals we've landed and the projects we've completed. But if we want to be truly respected leaders who can connect with people, we should also be like Oyama and share some of the more challenging and authentic parts of our lives.

62

Another Tailor, Another Chef

Some managers have many people reporting to them, but that alone doesn't make them leaders. To be a leader, you must have willing followers: colleagues who believe in you and don't just obey you because of your rank. This requires the ability to motivate people by recognizing their strengths and digging deeper into the reasons behind their successes. It's natural to see the flaws in others (I've been guilty of this myself), but you need to understand the positive traits of your teammates, so you can offer them thanks and appreciation on a more meaningful level.

Recognizing peers who've done a good job helps you build better relationships quickly, and sets you up to become a future leader by establishing a valuable habit even before you have your own direct reports. Being more observant about people need not start in the workplace. Think about those you come across in your everyday life and how they got to where they are today.

Curious at the Circus

I was attending a Cirque du Soleil show in Hong Kong. As I watched the gravity-defying acrobatics, I wondered how much time and effort the artists had to put in to deliver such a spectacular performance. I thought about the intense focus they must have to ensure the safety of themselves and their teammates. I wondered how many times they must have fallen during their training before they could stand proudly in front of the crowd during the live event.

The show reminded me that having curiosity about others is also important at work. As a leader, when you see colleagues achieve a great result, you shouldn't just admire the end product; you should pay attention to the steps they took along the way. They will appreciate it if you go beyond praising them and take a genuine interest in their journey to success. How many times did they fail and learn from their setbacks? You won't know if you don't ask.

Fascinated by a Street Food Chef

In 2016 in Singapore, Mr Chan Hon Meng's humble soy sauce chicken outlet became the world's first street food stall to win a Michelin star. Although I'd read media reports about Mr Chan, I wanted to find out for myself how he'd achieved this accolade. I went to his eatery at lunchtime hoping to sample his food and ask him some questions. The queue was massive! But although I had no chance of getting my order in, Mr Chan kindly agreed to have a chat when he closed for the day. It was a fascinating discussion, after which I came up with a list of qualities that have helped Mr Chan become successful. For starters, he's hardworking, humble, friendly to customers, has a positive outlook, and is passionate about his ingredients.

I was particularly struck by how efficient he is. Working with just one helper in his stuffy stall, Mr Chan is an ultrasonic chopping machine churning out plate after plate of his signature chicken noodles. The not-so-tall chef has customized his workspace to ensure his chopping board and cooking table are at the optimal height. Mr Chan is also extremely professional. Most street food vendors wear T-shirts and shorts because of their hot and oily working environment, but Mr Chan puts on a neat white chef uniform every day. When I asked him why he still sells his meals for a few dollars, he replied that it's a fair price for the hawker center location he operates in. This revealed another one of his strengths: integrity. Mr Chan[1] hadn't taken advantage of his fame to increase prices for his loyal customers.

---

[1] His stall, Hawker Chan, lost its Michelin star in 2021.

A Tailor I Can Trust

I have two great tailors in Hong Kong: one for shirts, one for suits. For the past 15 years, all my work shirts have been made by Mr Chung. He has plenty of other regular clients, despite facing strong competition, not doing any advertising, and working from a small fourth-floor shop in an obscure Causeway Bay building that doesn't have a lift. How does he keep his customers happy? Like Mr Chan the chef, Mr Chung the tailor has several qualities that set him apart:

- His workmanship is of a high standard. While most tailors just take your measurements and get someone else to do the stitching, Mr Chung does everything himself — from the cutting and sewing, to the final adjustments.
- He's industrious. He's usually at work even if I call him on a weekend.
- He always delivers on time.
- He pays attention to details. He makes my left cuffs slightly bigger than my right ones to allow room for my Timex watch.
- He can be trusted. It takes me only a minute to order my shirts over the phone, but I know he'll get everything right.

There are many unsung heroes like Mr Chung among us, if we're curious enough to recognize their expertise. We should spend a little time observing them, and think about why they've been able to achieve success in their fields. Once you get into this routine, you can bring it into the workplace. If you aspire to be a good leader, you'll want to have curiosity, so you can discover the strengths in others. This takes more than saying a token "great job" to someone and leaving it at that; it typically means talking to them to understand their hard and soft skills, and how they contribute to the success of the team.

As a leader, you can't always use your job title to get people to do things, and your firm will probably restrict the pay rises and promotions that you're able to hand out as motivational tools. But when your team members receive some genuine recognition of their abilities and achievements, they'll feel more connected to you and more willing to stick around when your company is going through tough times.

63

How to Be a Community Leader

Becoming a leader in your company can be a long and arduous process, especially if you've only recently graduated. Even as you get older, you won't always secure those big promotions you think you deserve. So don't wait years for your employer to make you a leader; take the opportunity to become one yourself — outside of the office.

You could do this by going for a leadership role in an established organization like an alumni association or sports club, but you're likely to face strong competition from others vying for the same position. Another way to groom yourself as a leader is to create your own community and nurture it, so that it gives you new skills and exposes you to senior people. The good news is that you can do this as a student or junior employee — age is no barrier. With that in mind, here's a six-point plan to becoming a leader in a community of your choice.

Choose Your Focus

Your community should be centered around a topic that you think you'll be interested in over the long term. Three young people I know have set up communities in fields that excite them: Jason, a business school student, is passionate about managing personal finance; Candy, a recently graduated industrial designer, hopes to leverage her design skills to help her community; and Charles, an engineer who has completed a few marathons, is interested in promoting health and fitness.

Start Small

Some people I talk to about community leadership are too scared to get the ball rolling because they think it requires serving a big market. But if you want to gain leadership skills, it's best to start small and target a narrow, accessible and engaged audience: 10 to 20 people is fine. Jason's personal finance group is made up of his schoolmates, who want to learn how to manage their money when they graduate. Candy has created a small LinkedIn group to help non-designers create beautiful posters and infographics for social media. And the fitness fanatic, Charles, isn't trying to convince fellow gym bunnies to do the next Ironman triathlon with him; he just wants to encourage a few exercise-shy office workers to get healthier.

Use Social Media

Make use of social media to build and lead your new community. Personal finance guru Jason concentrates on posting on Instagram because it's the most popular platform among his young peers. Candy mainly uses LinkedIn because she wants to network with professionals, while Charles, the super-fit engineer, is building his wellness community by creating a Facebook group. Social media also allows you to scale your community online. When you gain some momentum, you can invite work colleagues who share your interests to join your community. This is a great opportunity to show them your leadership qualities.

Find Your Partners in Crime

You don't have to lead everything by yourself. Partnering with other people from the outset makes running your community easier and more fun. You can divide up the workload according to your areas of expertise. You could concentrate on engaging with community members, while your friend does the marketing and takes photos during online and offline events.

Invite Senior Experts

Be part of a bigger network that can help your community. Bring in guest experts to interact with people in the group, such as through a

255

video conference, casual lunch, or networking event. If you're leading a community for budding amateur videographers, for example, try reaching out to a professional video expert. You may be surprised by your newfound ability to attract senior people in your field. Once you've established yourself as a strong community leader, other leaders will respect you and be more willing to help you.

Teach

You'll eventually build up enough knowledge and confidence to start teaching and coaching people in your subject. You could organize training webinars, offer classroom-style teaching, or coach people one-to-one. Whatever method you choose will elevate you to the status of a coach/ teacher, and will give you critical leadership skills in the process that will help you when you become a boss in your company. Managers are increasingly expected to be teachers rather than tyrants. They should be able to coach and inspire people in their teams who are struggling, not just focus their attention on the top performers.

When I was midway through my banking career, I began training small classes of younger colleagues in my specialist area, financial engineering. These people became my community. As a result, my boss started sending juniors to me for one-to-one coaching if he was worried about their performance. After proving myself as a teacher and coach, my manager told me that I was being groomed to take up a leadership position.

Leading your own community may not sound like a critical part of career success, but it can yield big results over time by establishing your leadership skills and marking you out as a leader both within and outside your company. It can help open doors to decision makers. When fitness-focused Charles started inviting his engineering peers to join him for group exercise sessions, managers at his firm were impressed that he'd already launched a successful community. One of them even wanted to participate. Senior leaders like connecting with young leaders.

When you've firmly established yourself as a community leader, you can look forward to becoming a thought leader. I'll tell you more about thought leadership in Chapter 64.

64

The Education We Need Next Year

You don't need a fancy job title to be a leader. Social media channels have given you a platform to become a thought leader outside your company. Being a thought leader requires you to have informed opinions, and to dedicate time and effort to your chosen area of expertise. You should be a go-to person in that field. But offering fresh perspectives and innovative ideas isn't easy.

Several years ago over Christmas, I wrote a post on LinkedIn titled, "The education we need next year". I published it at about 11 pm and went to sleep. When I woke up the next morning, I couldn't believe my eyes! My article had more than 1,000 comments, and the numbers of views kept increasing by the minute. I had been blogging on LinkedIn for a year and this article was my first viral post. It was a turning point for me in becoming a thought leader in education. Here's the full text of my article:

Yes, we still need mathematics, science and languages, but we also need life skills to live a more interesting and meaningful life. I have this big idea to start an Institute of Life (IOL). You still go to your regular school, but you attend IOL part-time online and we'll meet face to face once a year.

1. School prepares you for jobs; IOL prepares you for life.
2. School asks you what you want to be when you grow up (doctor, engineer, teacher etc.); IOL asks what problems you want to solve, and what skills you want to use.

3. School teaches you how to defend yourself from school bullies; IOL teaches you how to defend yourself from office politics.
4. School teaches you hard sciences; IOL teaches you soft skills.
5. School organizes storytelling competitions; IOL wants to hear your personal stories.
6. School teaches you languages; IOL teaches you body language, how to read what is said and what is not said, and how to use photography as a language.
7. School teaches you how to write reports; IOL teaches you how to write a blog.
8. School asks you to read Shakespeare; IOL asks you to read Malcolm Gladwell.
9. School teaches you marketing; IOL teaches you personal branding.
10. School organizes sporting events; IOL tells you why sitting can be bad, and gives you tips to keep your spine healthy and your waistline intact, so that you can still dance at a nightclub when you reach 50 without pulling a muscle.
11. School may give you so much homework that you have no time for anything else; IOL shares extreme time management tips, so you have time for everything else.
12. School gives you an environment to network on campus; IOL introduces like-minded people to you for networking online.
13. School gives you assignments; IOL gives you assignments too — assignments to write a LinkedIn post and create a video CV.
14. School gives you exams and sees if you pass or fail; IOL trains you to stand up after you fall.
15. School talks about work-life balance; IOL talks about work-life integration.

Taking Criticism as a Thought Leader

My article was successful because it offered a fresh perspective on education and therefore might have helped me demonstrate my thought leadership. However, it also expressed potentially controversial ideas. As someone new to blogging, it took courage to publish this post because I was wary of negative comments. Sure enough, I received some. These are just two examples:

"Interesting... but I disagree with you on the description of today's schools. In Sweden, we prepare students for real life... we've had those IOL thoughts for many years."

"Eric that's funny. You mean to say that your life skills were not learned in school? How about the ability to ask a question? I truly disagree with your concept of what school is."

This kind of feedback initially made me doubt myself. I've since learned that if you want to be consistently successful as a thought leader, you should be more worried about a lack of criticism than an abundance of it. If everyone agrees with you and you don't get any pushback, this suggests your ideas aren't interesting enough and have made little impact on your readers.

It can be daunting to be a thought leader on social media because you open yourself up to being challenged in a public forum. But you must learn to welcome online criticism and not be afraid of it. Unless it's abusive or harmful, you shouldn't delete or ignore it. Constructive criticism encourages more engagement with your social posts as your followers respond to each other's opinions. Reading viewpoints that differ from your own can also make you more informed as a thought leader.

From Thought Leader to Company Leader

The thought leadership skills you acquire by posting engaging content on social media or by speaking at events can help you prepare to be a leader in the workplace. The ability to inspire people by offering fresh perspectives on important issues (a core part of thought leadership) is also important as you become more senior and take on decision-making responsibilities in your job.

If you can't cope with criticism, you won't be effective in a job that requires you to lead people. As a leader, you'll inevitably have colleagues and clients who challenge you. Social media provides an excellent training ground to effectively handle and learn from negative feedback. When someone criticizes one of my LinkedIn posts these days, I don't get upset. I see it as an opportunity to broaden my horizons and become a better leader.

65
What I'd Tell My 22-Year-Old Self

As a leader, it's tempting to focus on building relationships solely with the more senior and influential people in your company and your industry. But in doing so, you overlook the junior professionals who may prove just as important to your career over the long term.

Why You Need a Junior Network

The ability to groom young talent is a core element of successful leadership. Offering advice to interns and recent graduates in your company will single you out in their minds as a leader. They may be unsure about aspects of their jobs and will be grateful for your help. You will retain a strong reputation as a leader as they climb the corporate ladder. Talking to your junior colleagues is also a good way to learn first-hand about the latest technology trends that their generation is embracing.

Don't just forge relationships with young people in your own company. There will be times when you need to take on junior employees or start a team from scratch as you react to disruption in your industry. Hiring drives like this will proceed more smoothly if you have an established network to tap. I'd recommend keeping an ongoing list of people, including juniors, who respect you and may want to work for you one day. Like a football manager considering which young players to recruit, you need to keep track of people whose skills will complement your team. After all, your effectiveness as a leader ultimately depends on how strong your team is.

How to Build Relationships With Younger People

How do you get young people on your talent list and make sure they stay there? Before they help you (e.g. by joining your team) you need to help them. As the more senior person, the best way of doing this is to offer them life and career advice that will establish a mentor-like relationship. As someone with more experience, however, it's not always easy to know exactly what to say to a young professional. What kind of information and insights will really benefit them? When we've been working for a few years, we sometimes forget what it's like to be just starting out. To put you on the right path, I suggest writing a letter to your younger self to offer a few life lessons.

Eric's Letter to Young Eric

I've written the following note to my 22-year-old self. As an engineering student, I wasn't particularly confident, and my focus was on school work and not much else. If I could travel back in time, I'd offer the following five tips:

Think "Crazy"

Eric, your life is a little boring. You need to think a bit "crazier" and do more fun stuff. Why not organize big cultural events and parties at your school? On your own you're nobody, but by using the university's name you could attract sponsors to your events. Don't worry, students will turn up. Because you like design, why not ask your dean if you can take some elective courses at the Faculty of Architecture? Don't be afraid to take some risks!

Don't Accept "No"

Eric, changing people's mind isn't as difficult as you think. Don't wait until you're older to realize this. Don't accept "no" without putting up a fight.

Believe in the Butterfly Effect

Eric, you'll find that a small action you take today can have huge consequences later on (a phenomenon known as the butterfly effect). If you don't write an unsolicited letter to a bank's HR department, you probably won't get into banking. If you don't get into banking, you won't have enough money to do your masters in the U.K., and that also means you may not develop an international outlook and career. Believe in the butterfly effect: take action today, no matter how small that action is.

Learn Presentation Skills

Eric, your presentation skills are weak. Whether you set up your own company or work for someone else, you'll find that you'll need to make effective presentations. Unfortunately, these skills aren't taught in school, so engage in activities beyond the classroom to develop them.

Collect Failure Stories

Eric, you'll fail and be rejected time and again. An airline will reject your job application, Princeton will reject your PhD application, clients will reject your product recommendations, and your boss will turn down your request for promotion. Don't take setbacks too hard, as long as you have tried your very best. Failures are painful and make you lose confidence, but they also make you a more experienced and resilient person. Learn from failures and move on. Collect your failure stories because one day when you become successful, they'll make your conversations much more interesting.

Eric, at 22, you can do a lot more than you think. In the next few years, you may feel a little lost, but you can still lead an interesting life. I hope these tips offer you some direction. Enjoy the journey!

Becoming a Better Leader

Writing a letter like this will help you better understand the needs of people younger than you. It may also motivate you to kickstart your junior networking. You could return to your alma mater to give a talk, take interns at your firm out for lunch, become a mentor, or share your skills by running a training session in the office. However you go about helping and encouraging young people, they'll be grateful to you, and you'll be on your way to becoming a leader people want to work for.

66
Think Big

The ability to "think big" is a critical element of successful leadership, whether we're leading other people to greatness or trying to accomplish great things in our own lives. For me, thinking big is about coming up with momentous ideas that might bring about fundamental change.

There's little downside to thinking big. You need not reveal your grand plans to anyone, if you're worried about the naysayers. Nor do you need a step-by-step plan to steer yourself to glory. Achieving something truly significant typically takes a long time, and reaching your desired destination is a bit like sailing a boat. The wind will shift direction along the way, so you'll have to adapt to new environments, take advantage of unexpected opportunities, and not adhere rigidly to a fixed plan.

You need to start somewhere, however. And that means taking an immediate and relevant small action to begin your journey. Without seizing the moment, your thoughts will remain just thoughts. I've tried to put my big ideas into action many times over the past 20 years. Although thinking big hasn't always yielded the results I expected, it's taught me some important lessons about myself, and sometimes it's changed the course of my life.

Architect

Think big: Become an architect

Small action: Apply for an architecture degree

Outcome: Although I'd wanted to become an architect since high school, I wasn't confident enough in my creative abilities to pursue a degree in architecture. I instead did engineering for my bachelor's and finance for my master's. But I couldn't let go of my dream. After 10 years of working in banking, now in my mid-30s, I sent in an application to the architecture faculty of a university in Singapore. This small action kick-started a chain of events. The department invited me to take a test and I tried my best to draw some of my own designs. To my surprise, I was offered a place on the course.

I was all excited on the day I received the acceptance letter, and couldn't get to sleep until late that night. Just thinking about the design courses I'd be taking made me so happy. But then I started calculating the opportunity costs. It would take about six years to train and qualify as an architect. If I stayed in banking during that same period, I'd be promoted at least once and earn enough money to buy another property. The next morning, I put on my suit and went to the office. I continued to work in banking for the next 10-plus years, and never became an architect. Whenever I walk past the iconic HSBC building in Hong Kong or Apple's spectacular dome-shaped store in Singapore (both designed by the famous architecture firm, Foster + Partners), I pause to ponder what life might have been like if I'd had the courage to make a career change.

Although I didn't become an architect, I've kept my interest in design alive. It has enriched my life, and allows me to relate to other people who are interested in design.

Marathon Runner

Think big: Run a marathon

Small action: Run 3km at the gym

Outcome: Completing a marathon would be a great achievement for someone who was physically weak in school. I wasn't an experienced long-distance runner, so I started small: I ran 3km on the treadmill at my gym. I then increased my distance by 1km every week until I reached 33km just a month before my (42km) marathon. Unfortunately an old slipped-disc problem came back at that point. Months of training went down the drain and I couldn't run in the marathon. Sometimes thinking big doesn't work out as you hope it will. But I'm still proud of my efforts: 33km is a milestone by my standards.

Blogger

Think big: Become a blogger

Small action: Write one short article on LinkedIn

Outcome: I'd always been fascinated by bloggers' ability to create interesting content. Wanting to become a blogger myself was a big deal for me. I hadn't been a confident writer since I failed my English exam back in high school. After worrying about where to publish and what my long-term strategy should be, I just decided to go for it: I posted one article on LinkedIn. I received some good feedback from readers, kept on writing, and after a year I started posting in Chinese too, which broadened my follower base. My audience grew again when I traveled to India and the Middle East to give speeches, and when I made online presentations to MBA and EMBA students at Oxford and Chicago Booth, respectively. One small action put me on the path that opened up all these opportunities.

Today I feel comfortable about my writing and honored to have so much engagement from followers around the world, which allows me to build connections with people, many of whom I've not met in person. My own life has been changed by the interactions I've had with my followers, and I always feel encouraged when people tell me that the small actions they've taken after reading my articles have led them to achieve big success.

The book you've just read is a consequence of me becoming a writer by posting that first LinkedIn article. Now you can see the power of small actions in your career and life.

Think big.
Start small.
Act now.

About the Authors

Rejected by Princeton for its PhD program, Eric Sim, CFA, PRM, was devastated he couldn't become an academic. He continued his banking career, working for Citi in Singapore, Shanghai and Hong Kong before joining UBS Investment Bank as a managing director. While in banking, he taught part time at the Hong Kong University of Science and Technology as an Adjunct Associate Professor of Finance, and at Tsinghua University as a guest lecturer. A key opinion leader on LinkedIn, Sim is now one of the most sought-after speakers and career coaches globally. He is the founder of Institute of Life, whose mission is to train young professionals to become successful at work and in life. A street food lover, Sim graduated from the National University of Singapore with an engineering degree, and from Lancaster University with an MSc in Finance. Read more about him on LinkedIn: linkedin.com/in/simeric/

Simon Mortlock is an experienced writer and editor, and an expert in producing B2B and B2C content across a range of digital channels, including articles, videos, webinars, ebooks, and white papers. He specializes in employment-related topics, and currently works as a Content Manager at eFinancialCareers (eFC), a website that empowers financial services and technology careers. Mortlock, who was previously the company's Asia Pacific Editor, joined eFC more than 10 years ago and has since been based in both Singapore and London. He has degrees in Law and History from the University of Auckland, as well as a Postgraduate Diploma in Journalism. Follow him on LinkedIn: linkedin.com/in/simonmortlockeditor/

Printed in Great Britain
by Amazon

72226964R00154